THE
HISTORY OF TH
HILL FAMILY
OF
OLDNALL, DENNIS, LYE,
Blaenavon, Bromsberrow, Broome, Clent, Felton, Foxcote, Heavitree, Hindley, Kidderminster, Madresfield, Malvern, Ocle Pychard, Oldswinford, Preston Wynne, Rock, Rugeley, Scalby, Sedgley, Shelsey Beauchamp & Worcester

RESEARCHED AND WRITTEN
BY
DON COCHRANE

Published by M. J. Cochrane

ISBN 978 0 9541753 4 4

Designed and type set by the author

Dedicated to my wife Margaret

Contents

THE HILL FAMILY OF OLDNALL, DENNIS AND OTHERS

	Page
Introduction & Prologue	
* John Hill of Oldnall (1667-1723)	1
* Joseph Hill of Stourbridge (1700-1735)	5
* John Hill of Foxcoat (about 1724-1758)	5
* Elizabeth (Hill) Batchelor of Colbornbrook (1703-1762)	5
* Thomas Hill of the Hamlet of Amblecote (1711-1782)	6
* Waldron Hill of Coalbourne Brook (1706-1789)	7
Edward Hill of Oldnall (1723- ....)	8
* Waldron Hill of Garden Market, Worcester (1730 – 1785)	8
Mary (Hill) Waldron (1732-....)	9
* Thomas Hill of Dennis (1736-1824)	9
* Melsup Hill of Dennis (1773-1824)	29
Sarah (Hill) Hopkins of Rugeley	29
* Samuel Hopkins of Blaenavon (1762-1815)	29
* Sarah Hopkins of Rugeley (1768-1844)	30
* Thomas Hill (2) of Broome (1767-1827)	36
Eliza Ann (Hill) Amphlett of Clent (1770-1837)	38
Thomas Hill (3) of Blaenavon (1790-1868)	39
* Waldron Hill of Broome and Heavitree (1775-1844)	40
Reverend Hopkins Hill (1811- ....)	40
* Reverend Charles Hill of Bromsberrow (1786-1856)	40
Reverend Reginald Pyndar Hill of Bromsberrow (1820-1887)	52
William Charles Hill of Bromsberrow (1831-....)	52
John Hill of Waterford (1749-....)	52
Penelope Hill of Wordsley (1778-....)	53
Francis Hill of Wollaston (1811- ....)	53
Sarah Hopkins Hill (1810-....)	54
Reverend Edward Hill of Hindley (1774-1853)	54
* Reverend Henry William Hill of Rock (1782-1840)	55
Reverend Henry Thomas Hill of Felton (1814-1882)	57
Reverend Walter Wilmot Hill (about 1844-1888)	61
Lieutenant Colonel Herbert Francis Hill of Scalby (1850-1911)	62
Captain Gerard Leader Hill (1882-1917)	63
Reverend Melsup Hill of Shelsey Beuchamp (1818-1887)	64
Marianne Hill of Rock and Shelsey Beuchamp (1827-1886)	65
James Charles Hill (1815- ....)	66
Reverend Thomas Hill of Foxcote (1772-1811)	66
Marianne (Hill) Brook of Oldnall (1804-.....)	66
Mary Penn (Hill) Bagley of Bagley's Mill (1763-....)	68
* Francis Hill (2) of Foxcote (1760-1835)	71
Melsup Hill of 'Laye' (1845-....)	73

*Will available

The Coat of Arms of Thomas Hill of Dennis 1736 -1824.

Motto: 'Esse Quam Videri' – 'To be rather than seem to be'

The pictures shown here are of Thomas Hill of Dennis (1736 – 1824) and his wife Anne Melsup. The original portraits, from which these digital pictures have been taken, belong to Mr. Godfrey Hill of Coventry, who is a descendent of Thomas Hill.

Thomas Hill was baptised 19th October 1736 at Kingswinford. He married Anne Melsup 22nd November 1766 at St. Andrew's Church, Holborn, London, she was the daughter of Henry Melsup, of London, and Mary Penn of Bromsgrove, she was born 22nd January 1742 and baptised 7th February 1742, at St. Dunstan's, East London.

The Digital pictures were taken by Clive Gardener of London.

Thomas was a Banker, Glass Maker, Iron Master, Coal Master and Clay Merchant, a Public Benefactor, provider of fourteen Schools, and two Churches.

Anne died 7th December 1810, aged 69, and Thomas died 17th September 1824, aged 87.

INTRODUCTION

After researching the history of Lye and Wollescote and finding the Hill family were benefactors of Lye and that their roots were at Oldnall in Lye, it was decided to take the research a little further and discover more about the family.

The history of the Hill family is a 'rags to riches' story, mixed with hardship and grief, not all made a fortune or left their mark in history, many died young, some whilst in their prime of life.

The Hills were a extraordinary family, well worthy of further research, but like all families, the Hills had no recognised beginning, and likewise, no recognised end, as family history does not begin at a specific point in time, or end at some other specific point either. Since the further back in time family research is taken, the poorer become the records, and the more uncertain become the facts, with that in mind, one has to be content with selected dates.

The biggest problem with the Hill family is its size, which makes it a formidable task to even attempt to construct a simple family tree, and impossible to provide documental information on every member of the family. Most of the family trees shown in this book, whilst having been drawn up as accurate as possible from records and family wills, do contain some inaccuracies and some intentional omissions.

A study of Genealogy, shows there was a general 'shortage' of Christian names in early times, these were either biblical, or taken from Royalty, or famous people. Family names were passed down using simple rules, which were not necessarily followed on every occasion. The first male child was usually named after his father and likewise with the first female child, who was usually named after her mother. Other names then tended to follow other members of the family and were repeated. This often led to confusion of Thomas one, two and three, or Mary one, two or three, as the reader will discover. Other Christian names, or second names, were given using the maiden name of the mother, or the surname of other relations, or close friends, this was a common practice used by the Hill family.

The Hills were staunch Anglicans, their names becoming associated with a number of churches, not only in and around Worcester, but also Hereford, Gloucester, Blaenavon and many other places.

Authenticity

Documents that have been transcribed and quoted here are reproduced as close as possible to the originals. Spelling, grammar, mistakes or other peculiarities shown on the originals have not been corrected.

Acknowledgements

I would like to thank the following for their help and assistance in the production of this book, The Public Record Office at Kew, Stourbridge Library, Dudley Archives, the various churches, which we visited, and are shown in this book, not all of them being open at the time of our visit, but were opened for us at our request. Harry Thornton of Rugeley, who I met by chance in Rugeley Library.

Prologue

On the "Four and Twentieth day of September 1695, and in the Seventh Year of the Reigne of our Sovereigne Lord William the Third by the grace of God of England Scotland France and Ireland Defender of the Faith". "John Hill, sithsmith", signed an Indenture for a two hundred year lease, from Lord Foley and the Feoffees of Oldswinford Hospital, for Oldnall House and Farm, together with numerous closes and pieces of land in the parishes of Oldswinford and Cradley, for "a yearly sum of Five and Thirty Pounds of good and lawful money of England".

The Hill family of Oldnall has its origins at Clent, and are shown in the Clent parish records as early as 1562, with the marriage of William Hill to Anna Rowleye 1st July 1562, and a later entry dated 22nd April 1577, was the baptism of Francis son of Abraham Hill and Agnes. Whilst there were no further entries for William and Anna Hill, there were more baptisms for the family of Abraham and Agnes including Adam 1579, John 1582, Henry 1583, Agnes 1587, Richard 1589, and Will 1593.

In the period from 1562 to 1700, there were approximately 281 Hills recorded in the Clent parish registers, they were the second largest family in Clent, the largest being the Waldron family. Of the 281 Hills entered, there were 48 Thomases, 44 Johns, 28 Abrahams, 32 Anns, 25 Elizabeths, 18 Marys, and numerous Williams, Richards, Francises, and Henrys, which were some of the most popular Christian names.

About 1659 Thomas Hill married Penelope ...... where and when this event took place, or the surname of Penelope is not known. They are recorded in the Clent records with the baptism of their first child Thomas in 1661, there then followed Joseph, John (of Oldnall) 1667, and Abraham.

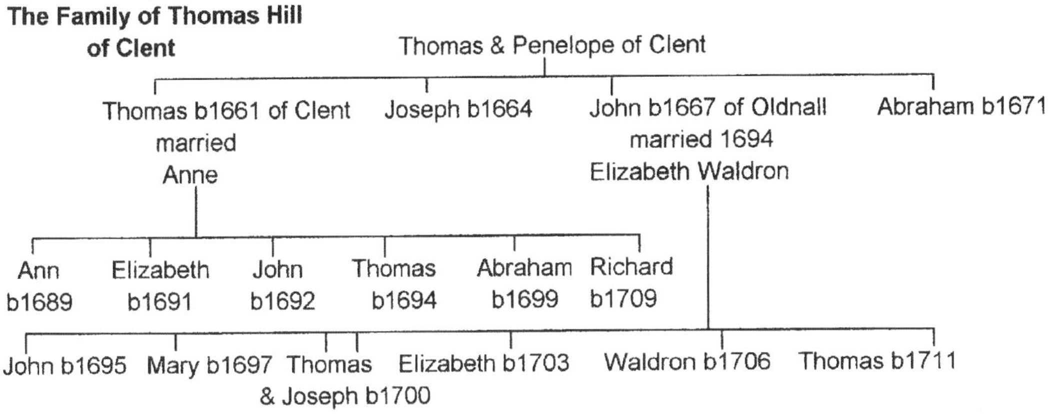

The early history of the Hills, at Clent, as shown in the parish records, did not suggest that many of them were moneyed, or ranked as having high status within the community; very few merited such titles as Gentleman, Gent, Master or Mr, which was often afforded to others.

Why John left Clent to come to Oldnall, is a matter of conjecture, perhaps the move offered him opportunities he could not find at Clent. Perhaps there were other unknown reasons. He was not the eldest son and, therefore, would not inherit his father's 'wealth or property', and opportunities to own his own farm or business at Clent, would probably be very remote, in a community with a rapid growing population, often spilling over into neighbouring parishes. Other factors, which may have influenced his move, could have been the presence of William Tristram, at Foxcote Farm, and John Amphlett of Clent, who also owned land in Wollescote.

John Hill of Oldnall (1667-1723)

John Hill was a farmer and scythesmith, his will made in 1723, shows evidence of his involvement in both trades. It is reasonably certain that John originated from Clent, but it is difficult to be absolutely sure, as there are overwhelming difficulties with the surname Hill, that offer many alternative routes in tracing their history, which might end up barking up the wrong family tree, and it is with that reason in mind, that the history of the family, shown in this book, begins in the late 17th century.

The marriage between John Hill and Elizabeth Waldron took place on the 2nd April 1694 at Chaddesley Corbett. The Waldron name was quite common in the area of Clent and Belbroughton, the family being involved in the manufacture of scythes. There was also a large number of Hills living in the same area, who were also involved in the manufacture of scythes, and there was at least three John Hills born at Clent between 1664 and 1668, who would be of the right marrying age, i.e. 20 to 30 years, the most favourable being John Hill born 1667 to Thomas Hill and Penelope. Elizabeth is thought to be the daughter of Thomas and Mary Waldron a scythe making family of Clent.

One other factor supporting the origin of the Hill family suggested above, although not proving it, is Bache's map of 1699, which shows the Tristram family occupying Foxcote Farm, Oldnall, which was the name of a Belbroughton family. Other names in the will of John Hill point in the direction of Clent or Belbroughton.

The earliest mention of John Hill is the baptism of his son John in 1695 at Oldswinford. Other family members baptised by John and Elizabeth Hill at Oldswinford, include Mary 1697, Thomas & Joseph, twins 1700, Thomas died aged nine and was buried at Clent, 5th September 1710, Elizabeth 1703, Waldron 1706, and Thomas 1711.

A later mention in the "The Heraldry of Worcestershire" by H. Sydney Grazebrook, list a number of land owners, at Oldswinford, in 1703, including, William Tristram, Gent, William Tristram, jun, and John Hill, Scythe Smith.

A further mention of John Hill of Oldnall is in the will of Thomas Pargeter of Park Side, Two Gates, who died in 1730, when John signed as a witness, signing as John Hill of Oldnall. Another reference can be found in the bounds of Oldswinford, made in 1733, which make reference to land at Oldnall[1] owned or leased by the Hills. Unfortunately, both these two references were of John Hill the younger, the son of John Hill of Oldnall, who died in 1723, his will has only recently been discovered, which proves he was at Oldnall, when it was made in 1723.

Thomas, the youngest child of John and Elizabeth, was born 20th June 1711 and baptised 16th July 1711 at Oldswinford, Elizabeth, his mother, was buried twelve days later on the 28th July 1711, at Clent, and is recorded as *Elizabeth wife of John Hill de Oldnall of the parish of Swinford.* The age of their children at the time of her death would be, John 16, Mary 14, Joseph 11, Elizabeth 8, Waldron 5, and Thomas about five weeks.

---

[1] Map Ref SO 932 839

The will *(PRO Prob 11/596)* of John Hill contained the following instructions, "I John Hill the Elder of Oldnall in the Parish of Oldswinford in the County of Worcester Scythe Smith being very sick and weak in body but of perfect mind and memory thanks be to God therefore calling to mind the mortality of my body and knowing that it is Appointed for all men once to dye doe make and ordain this my last will and Testament that is to say principally and First of all I give and Recommend my soul into the hands of God that gave it and for my body I commend it to the Earth to be buried in a Christian like and decent manner at the direction of my Executors nothing doubting but at the General Resurrection I shall Receive the same & again & by the mighty power of God and as touching such worldly goods and Estate where with it hath pleased God to interest me with all in this world".

To his son Thomas Hill, he left the "sume of Twenty pounds also he hath the lease of all Halfemore farm for ninety-nine years".

He bequeathed to his daughter Elizabeth Hill, three hundred pounds to be paid her one year after she became of age, and "five pounds She shall have paid that year but this is to let you know that if She Marry contrary to my brother Richard Waldrens[1] and my Sister Mary his wife and my son John Hills consent she shall have onely ten pounds paid her yearly for her life".

He gave to his son Waldron Hill, "Three hundred pounds to be paid him one year after the age of twenty one" and "ten pounds to be paid him yearly from my decease till then and when he marrys let him take care as above for otherwise he shall Speed the same with his Sister".

To his son Joseph Hill, he gave "three hundred pounds to be paid him one year after my decease provided and upon condition that my three Friends mentioned do jointly agree to it but if he should Marry Foolishly and without their advice and consent he shall have only Four pounds a year for his life and one hundred pounds but he shall have ten pounds paid him for the deads year or if he doth act Foolishly or Rubbishly in any other way besides Marrying he shall not have his whole money".

He left to his son-in-Law, Dolphine Munn, "one Shilling and no more to be paid him within Six months after my decease". He makes no mention of his daughter Mary, who, it appears, may have married against his wishes, or she has died.
A Dolphine Munn married Mary Hill, 7th June 1720, at St. Phillip's Birmingham.

To his eldest son John Hill, he left all his "Messuages Tenements Lands and Hereditaments Trade shop Tools Household Goods Cattell and Chattells", adding that "if he shall dye leaving noe issue able to manage the Trade", he wanted his Trade and Shop Tools to pass to his son Waldron Hill "whom I bred up in the same Trade and business".
He left Forty Shillings each to his four Younger Children, to buy each of them a bed.
His will was made 19th September 1723.
Witnesses *Wm Tristram. Henry Waldron. Eliz Tristram.*

---

[1] Care should be taken when interpreting relations mentioned as brothers, brothers-in-law and son-in-law, as they might not have quite the same meaning as today. Richard Waldron was the brother of Elizabeth. Clent school was built in 1704, on the site of a cottage where a Richard Waldron had previously been living.

John Hill made his will the 19th September 1723, and his burial is recorded in the Clent Parish records as 11th January 1723, both these dates are correct. At this particular time we were using to the Julian calendar, which started the New Year on the 25th March, and ended on the 24th March. In 1752 the calendar was changed to the Gregorian calendar, which is the system we use today, resulting that in the year 1751 there was no January, February or 24 days in March!

The burials of John and Elizabeth are proof that they came from Clent.

We can assume the witnesses, William Tristram and Eliz Tristram, were from Foxcote Farm, and since a William Tristram married his cousin Elizabeth Waldron, at Clent, 30th April 1692, it seems logical to think that they are related to Elizabeth Hill.

Later, the Hills owned and occupied Foxcote Farm, but there are no records available of when this took place.

Henry Waldron, witness, was a scythe maker from Walton Clent. His will, made 1726, was witnessed by William Waldron. 'Henry Waldron, Gent' was buried, 9th November 1728, at Clent. A Henry Waldron was a Church Warden in 1675.

Elizabeth Waldron, was born at Clent to Thomas and Mary Waldron, in 1671, her brother Richard, was born 1679,

A Richard Waldron married a Mary Mun, 27th October 1702, at Dowles, Shopshire, which seems to create more questions than what it provides answers!

Halfemore Farm is thought to be the farm in Uffmoor, or Houghmoor Lane, Halesowen, which is shown on the 1834 map as being in Shropshire. Halfemore is now unknown in Clent, although it is mentioned at least twice in the parish records.

William Tristram, the Elder, of Old Swinford, made his will *(PRO Prob 11/479)* 3rd June 1702, he mentions his children, William, Thomas and Mary Penn. He describes himself as a Yeoman, and was obviously a farmer, from items mentioned in his will, and he appears to be living at Foxcote, we can assume this is the Tristram at Foxcote Farm, shown on Bache's map of 1699, and since a William Tristram witnessed the will of John Hill in September 1723, who was the son of William Tristram the Elder, mentioned above who died in 1704. William the Elder, left to his wife Mary, partly by a marriage settlement, and partly by his will, for her life time, which would then pass to his three children. He bequeathed to his wife, "six gold guinea pieces now in her owne custody one feather bedd with reed curtains pewter dishes and plates brass candle sticks flaxen sheets and napkins his steele malt mill and his largest iron grate standing in the kitchen also one of his best cowes malt corne grain in the barne and all my muck and compost", of which, the later two items must have been a valuable commodity in these times! He names his three children as his Executors.

William Tristram, the Elder, was the son of the Rev. Thomas Tristram of Belbroughton and his second wife, he was said to have invented the first round glasshouse, and to have greatly improved the art of making flint glass and purifying iron for making steel.

Thomas, the son of William Tristram, was the Rector of Allesley, near Coventry, from 1692 to1723.

A John Hill and a Thomas Tristram,[1] were two of the trustees of Oldswinford Workhouse, in 1733.

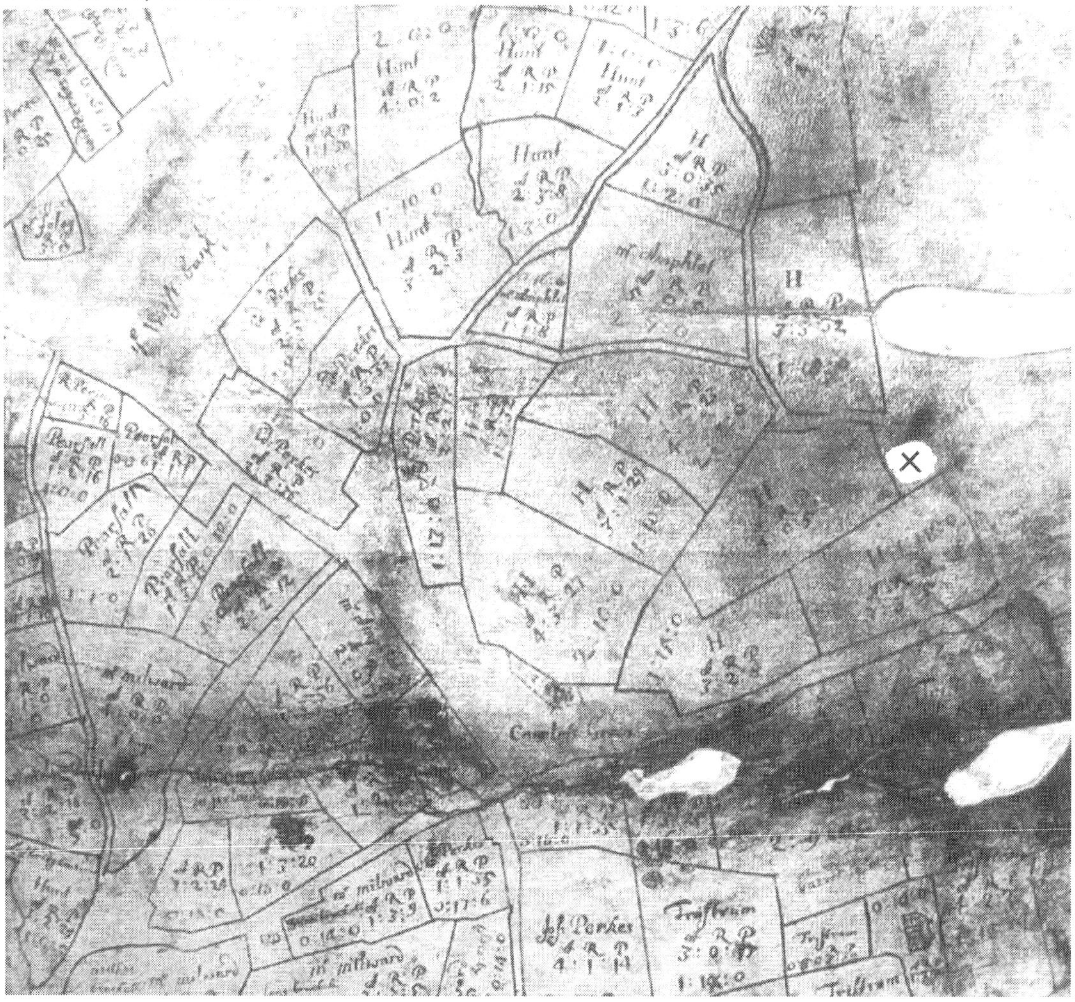

Bache's map of 1699, shows Foxcote Farm in the bottom right hand corner, with the land around it owned by Tristram. Wynall Lane is in the bottom centre, with Careless Green just above, Oldnall House and Farm, would be about where the **X** is, half way up the map on the right, with the surrounding land belonging to it, marked with an H for Hospital School. The land of Careless Green House and the Hare and Hounds, is shown belonging to Joseph Perks. Lye Waste is the clear area of land in the top left hand corner. The blank area top right, is in the parish of Cradley. The two roads leading up to Oldnall, from Balds Lane, are ancient roads, which did not get adopted into the present day road system, note also, land owned by Amphlett of Clent inside the triangle formed.

Mary, the daughter of William Tristram, married William Penn, at Broome Church in 1693, he was born at Chaddesley Corbett in 1656, and was described as a yeoman, he held the mortgage of the Heath Glasshouse, in Stourbridge, and lived at Harborough Hall, Hagley. Their daughter Anne, born 1702, married Thomas Shenston of the Leasowes, Halesowen, and was the mother of William Shenston, the poet and landscape artist.

---

[1]See " A HISTORY OF STOURBRIDGE" by Nigel Perry.

Joseph Hill of Stourbridge (1700-1735)

Joseph Hill, a Mercer of Stourbridge, was the surviving twin son of John Hill of Oldnall and Elizabeth Waldron, made his will *(PRO Prob 11/672)* in 1734, which was proved in 1735, his only son, Waldron, would be five years of age. He left £400 to his wife Hannah Allso, for her benefit, which was to pass to his son on her death. Thomas Milward and Thomas Hill were witnesses to his will, his wife Hannah, and his uncle Richard Waldron, were joint Executors.

John Hill of Foxcoat (about 1724-1758)

John Hill, was the son of John Hill[1] and Elizabeth Dillard, and grandson of John Hill of Oldnall, he was born about 1724. He died in 1758, leaving a will naming seven of his twelve brothers and sisters, but not his wife, only referring to her as 'my dear wife', who was Executrix and John Hill, his father, Executor. His will *(PRO Prob 11/838)* was proved 1st June 1758, when his wife, Elizabeth, was mentioned by name. Oldswinford records show a John Hill married an Elizabeth in 1756. He gave £500 and the interest to his father during his life, after which, the principal sum was to be divided as follows, £75 each to his sisters **Elizabeth** and **Martha**, £75 each to brothers **Thomas** and **Ambrose**, £100 each to brothers **Waldron** and **George**, to be paid six months after the death of his dear wife.
He gave £300 and an annuity of £20 to his wife. He makes no mention of any children in his will, but he states that he is a scythesmith, following the trade of his father and grandfather, and continues "I desire that my brother **Francis Hill** to have the benefit of the trade of a scythesmith which I have carried on". One other notable fact, is that he lives at Foxcoat. Witnesses were Francis Hill and Thomas Milward.

When the Tristrams left Foxcote Farm, or when the Hills took it over, is not known.

Elizabeth (Hill) Batchelor of Colbornbrook (1703-1762)

Elizabeth was the second daughter of John and Elizabeth Hill of Oldnall, who, from the tone of her father's will, had a strict upbringing.

One wonders if John's children took heed of the warning in his will, and in particular his daughter Elizabeth, who married a rich glassmaker of Stourbridge.

In 1725, one year after her father's death, Elizabeth married Humphrey Batchelor, who was the owner of glasshouses, land and property in Amblecote. Their son Thomas was born in 1727, and their daughter Mary, in 1732.

Humphrey died in 1741, and was buried 26th November, leaving Elizabeth with a fourteen year old son and a nine year old daughter, two glasshouses, a large estate called Dennis, in Amblecote, and property at Lichfield. Elizabeth successfully ran the business, known as Mrs. Batchelor's glassworks, with the assistance of her brothers Waldron and Thomas, who were Executors to the will of Humphrey, trustees and guardians to her children. The will *(PRO Prob 11/720)* of Humphrey also

---

[1] No will has been found for this John Hill, who was living in 1762 at the time of the death of his sister Elizabeth Batchelor.

carried a warning, similar to that given in the will of John Hill to his children, that if **Thomas** or **Mary** should marry before the age of twenty-four, without the consent of Elizabeth, uncle Waldron and uncle Thomas, their legacy of three hundred pounds would be reduced to fifty pounds "and no more"! One can almost see Elizabeth dictating his will.

Her son Thomas died in 1750, aged twenty-three, leaving Elizabeth on her own once more. Mary, her daughter, died some time after the death of Humphrey and before the will *(PRO Prob 11/881)* of Elizabeth was made.

Elizabeth Batchelor died in 1762, leaving all her business and trade affects in trust for her brothers Waldron and Thomas and their assigns, including farm lands etc.

To her brother, **John Hill** of Oldnall, she left £200, and to each of his eight children, she left "£100 apiece".
To her sister-in-law, Hannah Hill, widow, wife of Joseph, one hundred pounds and twelve pounds per year during her natural life, and to her "kinsman" Waldron, nephew, son of Joseph and Hannah, two hundred and fifty pounds.

She left "that Messuage or dwelling late Captain Bradley's with gardens and stables" (Dennis Estate) to her brother Waldron Hill, and Thomas was to receive £60 for his part of the house before any "obliteration" was made by his brother Waldron.

It would appear from the last paragraph above, that the Dennis Estate was originally left to Waldron, who intended to demolish the existing building and build a new house. After the death of Elizabeth, Thomas became the owner and he rebuilt it to become Dennis House.

Humphrey Batchelor is buried with his wife Elizabeth and their two children, on the north side of Oldswinford Church, most of the wording on the head stone is eroded and illegible.

Thomas Hill of the Hamlet of Amblecote (1711-1782)

Thomas and Waldron Hill, brothers to Elizabeth Batchelor, inherited the Fimbrell Glasshouse and the Coalbournhill Glasshouse, together with other properties from Elizabeth. Thomas rebuilt the near derelict house at Dennis, which became known as Dennis House, that he left to his nephew Thomas Hill, who called it Dennis Hall.

In his will *(PRO Prob 11/1089)* he left his farm called Halfmoor Estate, in the parish of Clent, to William Waldron of Stourbridge, glass merchant, and Thomas Waldron of Field House, Clent, in trust for his nephew Thomas Hill of Dennis, for the term of his natural life, to receive and enjoy the rents, it was then to pass to his eldest son. He left Fifty Guineas to Mary Dixon, Five Guineas to widow Waldron of Hagley, the same to the widow of Henry Bonar, widow of the Rev. Male, widow of John Hill of Foxcote, and the widow of Thomas Russell. Five hundred pounds to his niece Mary Waldron, wife of William Waldron, and the same to Sarah Hopkins, wife of Thomas Hopkins of Cannock Wood Forge, own master. £500 to William Waldron of Stourbridge, Francis Hill of Foxcote, and Thomas Hill of Dennis, in trust, with the yearly interest paid to his niece Martha (Hill) Blick, wife of Richard Blick, for her sole and separate use, and

after her decease, to her nephew Thomas Hill, son of Francis Hill of Foxcote. To his cousin, William Waldron of Stourbridge, he bequeathed 100 Guineas, and £500 to his brother Waldron Hill, with £300 to his nephew John Hill of Kingswinford, and £200 apiece to his two children, Edward and Penelope, when they reach the age of Twenty-one years. To his nephew Francis Hill of Foxcote, he left £1500 at the rate of £500 per year, and released him from all his debts, and also released to him, all his securities. To his nephew Waldron Hill of Worcester, he left £500, with the condition, that if he had no children at the time of his death, the same would be left and divided among the children, or grandchildren, of his uncles John Hill and Waldron Hill "as he shall think proper". He left £15, to be divided amongst the poor inhabitants of Careless Green and the Waste, Lye and Amblecote, "as William Waldron and Francis Hill think right", and £130, or so much from, to bring in a clear annual sum of £6, to be used for educating and teaching to read, twenty poor children of the Waste, Lye and Careless Green, whose parents are unable to pay for such learning, such teaching to be continued for two years, from the age of 7 years, no child to be admitted who is not acquainted with his/her letters. He states that Thomas Hill of Dennis, his Executor, is acquainted to his intention, relative hereto, and leaves him to manage the children's education accordingly.
He bequeathed £100 and an annuity of £30, to his nephew George Hill, "paid in amounts as seen fit by his brother Francis Hill". To his sister-in-law Hannah, widow of Joseph, an annuity of £20, and to his nephew Waldron Hill of Worcester, an annuity of £30. To **Elizabeth** and **Penelope Smith**, he leaves £250 each, to be paid seven years after they reach the age of twenty-four, unless they marry. To Mary Waldron, niece, wife of William Waldron, an additional sum of 200 Guineas, for her care and civility during his illness, to his cousin Richard Hill of Clent and his brother Thomas Hill, £5 apiece, for the term of their natural lives. He also left small amounts of money to his workmen at Coalbournbrook Glasshouse.

John Amphlett[1] mentions 'Halfmore' and also Thomas Hill, when making reference to the allocation of 'kneelings', in Clent Church, when one was assigned to Thomas Hill for the use of his tenant of Halfmore Farm, who was William Mole in 1780, when Thomas made his will.

The farming side of the Hill family of Oldnall and Foxcote, had certain financial difficulties, having to borrow money from the more affluent members of the family, running up debts, which were often only cleared at the decease of the lender, and any legacy or annuity left by the deceased, was left in trust for them, with a stern warning to the trustees, to be careful with the administration and applying restrictions, almost like dictating from the grave.

Waldron Hill of Coalbourn Brook (1706-1789)

Waldron Hill married Sarah Badger, in 1729; they had five children, Mary, Joseph, Thomas, Waldron and Sarah. His wife Sarah died and Waldron remarried Elizabeth Tyzack, a widow in 1746; they had one son, John born 1749.

Waldron and Thomas Hill, inherited the Fimbrell Glasshouse and the Coalbournhill Glasshouse, from their sister Elizabeth Batchelor, and whilst they had no experience

[1] See 'A Short History of Clent' by John Amphlett, page 159.

of glass making, their main business being scythe making and farming, they gained valuable experience by assisting Elizabeth, as directed by the will of Humphrey, her husband, for which she rewarded them in her will.

Waldron Hill, his son Thomas and partner William Waldron, were known to have had four scythesmith workshops[1] on the site of the Coalbournhill Glasshouse in 1770 and 1784. Waldron Hill was also said to have a scythesmith's workshop at Tiled House.

Whilst it is on record that Waldron lived at the 'Tile House', he stated he was living at Coalbournbrook, when he made his will *(PRO Prob 11/1175)* 25th June 1782.
His will left mainly to his son Thomas Hill of Dennis, who was his sole Executor. He left £50, to his son-in-law, William Waldron, and £1720 in trust, with the interest paid to his daughter Mary Waldron, and £500 to his granddaughter Mary Waldron. To his son-in-law Thomas Hopkins, he left £50, and £1000 in trust, and the interest there from, to his daughter Sarah Hopkins, and legacies of £700, to his grandson Samuel Hopkins, and £500 to his granddaughter Sarah Hopkins. He left £500 to the children of his son John, and released him from all debts, dues and demands, he owed to him, on condition that John released him from a marriage settlement of £1500, previously agreed, otherwise he would revoke the £500 legacy, and the release and discharge of his debts. A codicil to the will, dated 13th December 1782, revoked the legacy, the release and discharge of the debts, he had previously made to his son John.

Edward Hill of Oldnall (1723-....)

Edward was the son of John and Elizabeth Dillard, he married a Mary ...... and they had a son Waldron, baptised 19th November 1745, at Oldswinford.

Waldron Hill of Garden Market, Worcester (1730-1785)

Waldron was the son of Joseph Hill and Hannah of Oldnall, who were Mercers in Stourbridge, where they owned a shop in the Corn Market and a number of houses, which passed to Waldron on the death of his mother, his father dying when Waldron was about five years of age. Waldron made his will *(PRO Prob 11/1133)* in 1783, consisting of thirteen sheets, and eight Codicils on a further six sheets, whilst living at Garden Market, Worcester. His will confirmed he was the son of Hannah, but makes no mention of his trade or profession, or if he was married or if he had any issue. The two hundred and fifty pounds left to him by his aunt, Elizabeth Batchelor, he now leaves to his cousin Francis Hill of Foxcote. The five hundred pounds legacy left to him by his uncle Thomas Hill, he now leaves as twelve legacies, following the instructions left by his uncle Thomas, £110 to his first cousin Mary Waldron, £60 apiece to Thomas Hill of Dennis, his Executor, Mrs. Sarah Hopkins, and Mrs. Francis Hill of Foxcote, £30 each to the two children of the late John Hill of Wordsley and the two children of Mrs. Elizabeth (Hill) Smith, and £10 each to Waldron Hill of Oldnall, and his brother George. £50 to the Baptist Church in Worcester, £10 to the same at Netherton, Dudley, £20 to the Lady Huntington Chapel at Worcester, and £5 to the Rev. John Wesleys meeting in New Street, Worcester. £40 between the nearest, and poorest relations, of his late uncle Richard Waldron. He leaves his wearing apparel to his uncle Phillip Allso, his mother's brother, or to be given to the poorest relations on

---

[1] See The History of Amblecote.

his mother's side, and One Guinea to the school at the Waste, to which his late uncle left a legacy, to be laid out in books. His house in Foregate Street, Worcester, was sold to provide the various legacies and annuities. His final instruction to his Executors, was that he wished to be buried in a frugal manner, after the source and manner of his late dear mother, and he wished to be buried in the same vault with her.

Mary (Hill) Waldron (1732-....)

Mary Hill, daughter of Waldron Hill and his wife Sarah, married William Waldron, 29th January 1764, at Oldswinford. He was a scythesmith and business partner, to her father Waldron and brother Thomas of Dennis. William Waldron was one of the scythe making family of Clent and Belbroughton, and a probable relation to Elizabeth Waldron, wife of John Hill of Oldnall, he was a land owner, glass maker, clay merchant and banker. She had one daughter **Mary,** who married John Baker.

The Waldron's were early industrialists, specialising in the manufacture of scythes and edge tools at Belbroughton, Clent and Chaddesley Corbett, where they acquired both wealth and respect. Their family home was 'Field House' at Clent. They are mentioned in the 'Heraldry of Worcestershire' by H.Sydney Grazebrook as follows, "WALDRON of the Field House, Clent and Belbroughton and Stourbridge as borne by Roger Waldron of the Gildes house, Belbroughton, living about 1650, who married the only daughter of Rev. Richard Tristram, by Anne, esquire, his first wife, daughter of James Perrott of Bell Hall esquire; and by William Waldron, of Stourbridge, banker, High Sheriff in 1795, whose only daughter and heiress, Mary, was married to John Baker, of Waresley. The Waldron's were also of the Field House in Clent for several generations. The name occurs very frequently in the Clent registers, the second entry in the register book, being the baptism of Dorothy ye daughter of John Waldron".

William Waldron died at Hagley, in 1806, leaving to his five grand children, **Thomas William Waldron Baker, Harriet Baker, Margaret Baker, Emily Baker,** and **Caroline Baker,** naming his brother-in-law Thomas Hill and Thomas Hill the younger, as his Executors.

Thomas Hill of Dennis (1736-1824)

Thomas Hill, was the son of Waldron Hill and Sarah Badger. He married Anne Melsup, in 1766. Thomas inherited Dennis House from his uncle Thomas in 1782, together with other property, he later renamed it Dennis Hall[1]. He joined his father in the glass industry, owning both the Fimbrell and Coalbournhill Glasshouses. They were later joined by William Waldron and were involved in various enterprises known as 'Hill, Waldron and Hill', including the bank on the corner of Coventry Street and High Street, Stourbridge, called the Old Bank.

Berrows Worcester Journal, 24th December 1812[2], reported that in October, Mr. Thomas Hill Esq., and Co's Bank, at Stourbridge, was robbed of £20 in silver.

---

[1] Map Ref SO 899 858
[2] See Criminal Ancestors 1787 –1868, page 10, by Don Cochrane.

The above news item, included in the main report of the murder of Mr. Benjamin Robins, at Dunsley, Kinver, who was shot by William Howe, who was later hung at Stafford, and his body hung on a gibbet, at the spot where he shot Mr. Robins.

The Old Bank on the corner of Coventry Street and High Street Stourbridge. In 1808 Thomas and his son, Thomas Hill of Broome, formed a partnership with William Robins, a coal master and Thomas Bates. The bank traded as Hill, Bate and Robins.

The Hills formed various partnerships over the three generations of Thomas Hills, including, Hill, Bate & Robins, Bankers – Hill, Hampton & Co. – Hill, Waldron, Littlewood & Hampton – Hill, Hampton, Harrison & Wheeley, in all cases the senior partner was always a Hill.

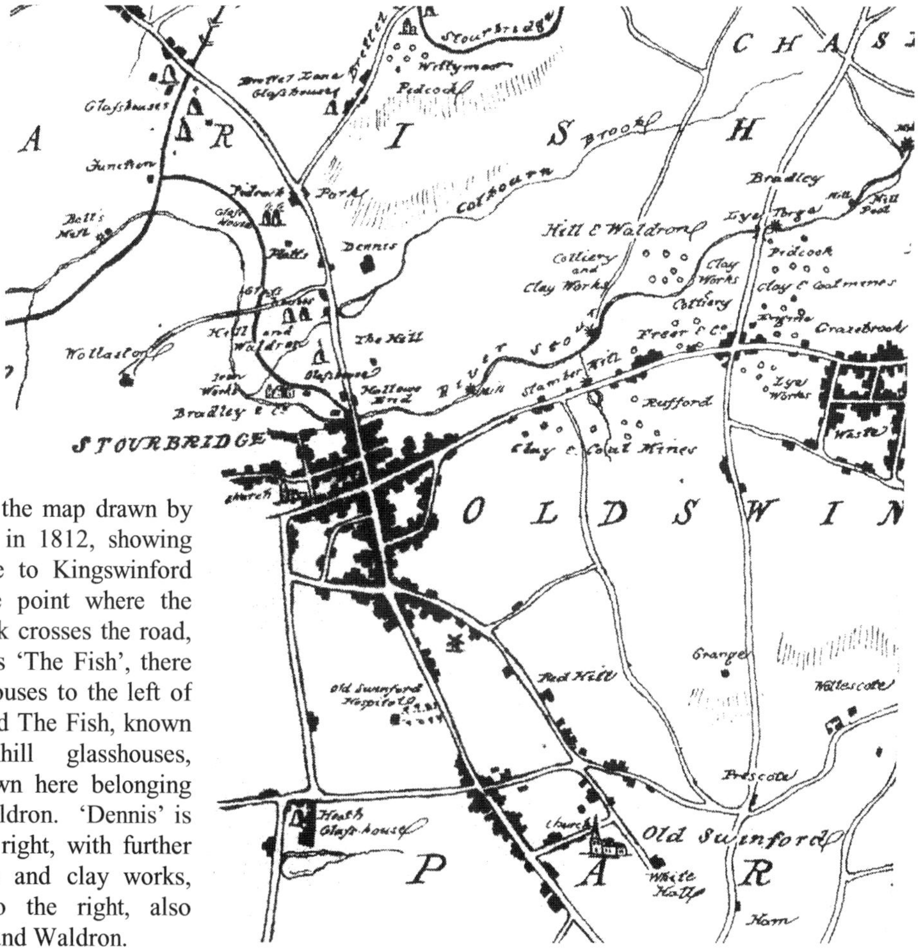

This is part of the map drawn by James Sherriff in 1812, showing the Stourbridge to Kingswinford Road. At the point where the Colbourn Brook crosses the road, known today as 'The Fish', there are two glasshouses to the left of the road, behind The Fish, known as Coalbournhill glasshouses, which are shown here belonging to Hill and Waldron. 'Dennis' is slightly to the right, with further land, collieries and clay works, still further to the right, also owned by Hill and Waldron.

The Coalbournhill Glasshouses at 'The Fish', around 1860, which were operated by the Hills until about 1835, when the Stevens family took over their occupancy. (Picture from the Stourbridge Library collection).

A previous map of Amblecote, drawn in 1774, by Robert Whitworth, shows a glasshouse on the opposite side of the road to 'The Fish', known as the Harlestones Glasshouse, and shown as Ensell & Hills Glass House, suggesting a partnership, whereas, Thomas Hill (1711-1782), owned it, and leased it to George Ensell[1].

Dennis Hall the home of Thomas and Anne (Melsup) Hill.

[1]See "Glassmakers of STOURBRIDGE AND DUDLEY 1612-2002", by Jason Ellis

About the Melsup Family

The Melsup surname name is most unusual; it is probably a corruption of the surname Melsop, which is also unusual. How Thomas Hill met Anne Melsup, is a matter of conjecture, with very little information available, and what information is available, is vague and skimpy, but interesting.

Henry Melsup married Mary Penn, 6th March 1736, at St. Helen, Bishopsgate, London. He died before the birth of his daughter Anne, leaving a brief will *(PRO Prob 11/720)* made, 5th November 1740, leaving everything to his wife, "and should she be with child or children to divide his estate amongst them". Witnesses to his will was Liell Gregg and Margaret Penn. His will was proved, 4th September 1742, with no codicils. His daughter Anne was baptised, 7th February 1742[1].

The will *(PRO Prob 11/796)* of Mary (Penn) Melsup, was made, 22nd March 1746, yet she made no provision for her daughter, which seems strange since Anne was only four years old. At this time the family was living at London. Her will was proved, 14th July 1752, six years later, with no codicils, Anne would now be aged ten years, so who looked after Anne?

The will of Mary gave more information about the family, than the will of her husband Henry Melsup. She named her cousin, Mr. Liell Gregg, of Tower Street, and Mr. Thomas Liell of Grevill Street, Holborn, as her Executors, leaving them twenty pounds each for mourning, and her sister, Margaret Penn, her Executrex, leaving her one hundred pounds, "and I give to my brother Mr. William Waldron of Stourbridge twenty pounds", the residue of her estate, she left in trust to Anne, until she became of age or married.

Margaret Penn, of Tower Street, in the parish of St. Dunstan's, Executrex and sister to Mary Melsup, died in 1755, three years after her sister. Her Will *(PRO Prob 11/816)* bequeathed twenty pounds to her brother William Waldron, and to her niece, Anne Melsup, she left all she possessed in public funds, her wearing apparel, money and rings. Her two houses in Bromsgrove, near to Dyers Bridge, she left to her cousin Elizabeth Watson, and a further house in Bromsgrove, next to the Golden Cross, she left to her cousin Liell Gregg.

From the above, a number of things maybe assumed, one, that Mary Penn originated from Stourbridge, or in that locality, and that her 'brother' was either a stepbrother or a brother-in-law? No evidence has been found to confirm either of the latter two assumptions. We do know that there was a strong family association between the Hills, the Waldrons and also the Penns, and to some extent the Tristrams. The name Mary Penn occurs on a number of occasions in this book.

So what did happened to Anne Melsup? We can only assume she lived with her aunt Margaret Penn, until she died in 1755, Anne would now be thirteen years of age, did she then come to live with her 'uncle' William Waldron, at Stourbridge, which gave her the opportunity to meet Thomas Hill, born 1736, and six years her senior?

---

[1] As previously mentioned, at this particular time we were using to the Julian calendar, which started the New Year on the 25th March, and ended on the 24th March, therefore, February came after March! The calendar was changed to the Gregorian calendar in 1752, which is the system we use today.

Possibly not, since they married, 22nd November 1766, at St. Andrew's Church, Holborn.

There were three Thomas Liells, the first mentioned above, died at Holborn, London, in 1774, his will *(PRO Prob 11/999)* left to his son, Thomas and his three daughters, shares in the South Sea Company and the East India Company, and twenty guineas to Anne and Thomas Hill, of Coalbourn Brook (Dennis).

The Melsup, Gregg and Liall Family Relationship

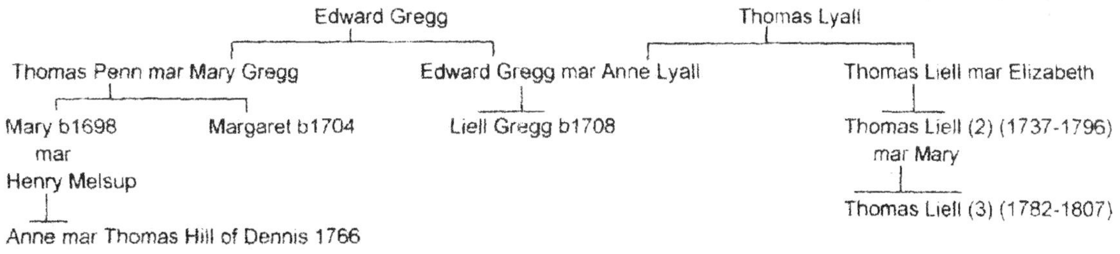

Thomas Liell (2), was the son mentioned above, born in Holborn in 1737, but died at Clent in 1796, and is named in the book, by John Amphlett, 'A Short History of Clent', as "a London merchant of the name of Liell who had bought the property of the Coxes, and built Old Clent Grove", which is said to be the site of the Sunfield Home. Thomas Liell (2), still held shares in the East India Company, when he made his will *(PRO Prob 11/1275)* in 1787, and also shares in the Stourbridge Canal Navigation and the Monmouth Canal Navigation Companies, his choice of investment in the latter two, was probably influenced by the advice of Thomas Hill of Dennis, who had an invested interest in both.

Thomas Penn was the grandfather of Anne Melsup, he married Mary Gregg in 1698, at Bromsgrove. He had two daughters, Mary, born 1698, and Margaret, born 1704, both baptised at Bromsgrove.

Edward Gregg, father of Mary, born Bromsgrove 1675, also had a son, Edward, baptised 1678, at Bromsgrove. Both the Penns and the Greggs, for some unknown reason, moved to St. Dunstan's, London, where Edward Gregg, the younger, married Anne Lyall in 1705, at St. Helen's, Bishopsgate, and had a son named Liell Gregg in 1708, and Mary Penn married Henry Melsup, in 1736, also at St. Helen's, Bishopsgate, and had Anne in 1742.

Anne Lyall had a brother, called Thomas (Lyall) Liell, who had a son, also called Thomas Liell (2), born in 1737, at St. Dunstan's, London, but died at Clent in 1796.

A marble memorial tablet, in the chancel of Clent Church, states that Thomas Liell (2), A.R.M., was a Lieutenant in the Royal Navy[1] and formally the commander of the 'Stafford East Indiaman', died in 1796, aged 58, his only son Thomas Liell (3), is remembered by a further marble tablet, died at Calcutta, in the East Indies in 1807, aged 25.

---

[1] The Liell family had a long history of seafaring; most of them held the rank of Captain and many of them were called Thomas. Records are available at a number of Archive offices.

The three daughters of Thomas Liell (2), Eliza, Mary and Anne, all died unmarried.

Thomas Liell (3), was in the 'Civil Service of the United Company of Merchants of England, trading to the East India and their Bengal Establishment' at Calcutta, where he died, his will *(PRO Prob 11/1488)* left almost everything he owned, to his sisters, Eliza and Mary. Anne, his younger sister, had died earlier, aged 15 years.

The two sisters, Eliza and Mary Liell, are remembered by a marble tablet in the chancel of Clent Church.

Edward Gregg, made his will *(PRO Prob 11/752)* 1st December 1745, appointing his son Liell, as his sole Executor, leaving to his niece, Mary Melsup, a one third share in a bond, of what appears to be a business, shared between himself, his son Liell and Henry Melsup, "provided that if she remarried she settled £500 on her daughter Ann". He left £50 to his niece Ann Melsup. His house in Bromsgrove, plus £100, he left to his niece Margaret Penn. He left his household goods, furniture etc., and £100 to his niece Mary Liell, £100 to his nephew Thomas Liell, and £40 each to his five chidren, and £25 to the charity school, for the benefit of the children of Tower Ward and Westham.

In 1787, Thomas Hill formed a partnership with Benjamin Pratt of Oldswinford, and his brother-in-law Thomas Hopkins, husband of Sarah Hill, in a venture at Blaenavon in South Wales, to build the first ironworks, of its kind, using technology that would revolutionise the production of iron, and make Thomas Hill a fortune.

All three partners were experienced iron masters. Thomas Hopkins, had an ironworks at Rugeley, on the Rising Brook, and Benjamin Pratt, occupied an ironworks at Wilden, near Stourport, powered by the waters of the river Stour, and also an ironworks at the Gig Mill Stourbridge, shown on Harry Court's map of 1782, powered by the brook that runs through Stourbridge Park.
Thomas Hill later occupied the Wilden ironworks, which was owned by the Foley family. In 1812, the Wilden ironworks was sold by auction[1], and said to be in the occupation of Thomas Hill, on a lease granted in 1801, he was also recorded as having a tin plate mill at the same site.

Wilden ironworks was later owned by Alfred Baldwin, who built All Saints Church, at Wilden, he was the father of Stanley Baldwin, (1867-1947), who was three times Prime Minister, 1923-24, 1924-29, and 1935-37.

Wilden Church was originally glazed with plain glass, which was replaced with fourteen stained glass windows, designed by the pre-Raphaelite artist, Edward Burne-Jones, who was related to the Baldwin family.

Iron from Thomas Hill's ironworks at Blaenavon, was brought by barge up the Severn estuary to Stourport, where it was either taken to his ironworks at Wilden, or continued, by canal into the Black Country, to the forges of the Stour Partnership.
It was at Stourport in 1818, that a Joseph Pritchard stole pig iron belonging to Mr Hill.

---

[1] See 'Wind and Water Mills' Number 4.

An engraving of the Ironworks in 1798, by William Bryne, from a drawing made by Richard Colt Hoare, which can be found in 'An Historical Tour in Monmouthshire' by William Coxe, published in 1801. (© Yale Centre for British Art, Paul Mellon Collection, USA/Bridgeman Art Library).

They leased 12,000 acres of land, at a cost of £1,300 per year, from Lord Abergavenny, which was rich in the raw materials, coal, limestone (flux) and ironstone, required for the production of iron, and could be found near the surface of the ground, and easily gathered from the Brecon Hills behind the works.

The hill behind the furnaces, was cut back to produce a vertical face, allowing the furnaces to be built against it, so that they could be easily charged at the top with raw materials. In front of each furnace was a casting house, with its floor covered with sand, in which a main channel, or runner was formed, and a number of other channels, set off at right angles, called sows, which branched off to form shorter, closed ended channels, called 'piglets'. When the clay 'plug' in the furnace was removed, the white-hot molten iron flowed down the runner channel, and into the branch channels to form pig iron or cast iron. Once cooled, the iron was broken into suitable lengths.

The draught or blast to the furnaces, was produced by means of a Boulton and Watt steam engine, which was considered at this time, to be at the 'cutting edge of technology'.

At first three furnaces were built, at a cost of £40,000, and employed 350 workers, working two shifts a day, of 12 hours, working one week on nights and one week on days, producing 3600 tons of cast iron per year, which increased to about 7800 tons in 1806.

Thomas Hopkins died in 1789, his share in the ironworks passing to his son Samuel Hopkins.

Two of the original casting houses as they are today.

Many of the important workers, were brought from the Black Country, where they were housed on site in linked type cottage accommodation, known as 'Stack Square', built around a large chimneystack. The houses, had segmental arched brickwork over the heads of windows and door frames, which was said to be a Midlands feature and unusual in Wales.

Stack Square, minus the stack, which became dangerous, and is now demolished. The three-storey building, on the extreme right, was the truck shop or Tommy Shop, where goods could be bought, often at high prices, but usually of inferior quality, i.e 'Tommy Rot'.

Workers were not always paid in cash; often they were paid by the truck system, usually in the form of tokens, with the employers name on them, which could only be spent in the company shop, these were known as Truck or Tommy shops. Some workers often ran out of food and money halfway through the week, and were allowed to purchase food or goods on credit, which had to be paid for the following payday out of their wages, resulting in some men having little or no wages after settling up.
The Anti-truck Act was introduced in 1831, but it was many years later before it came to an end.

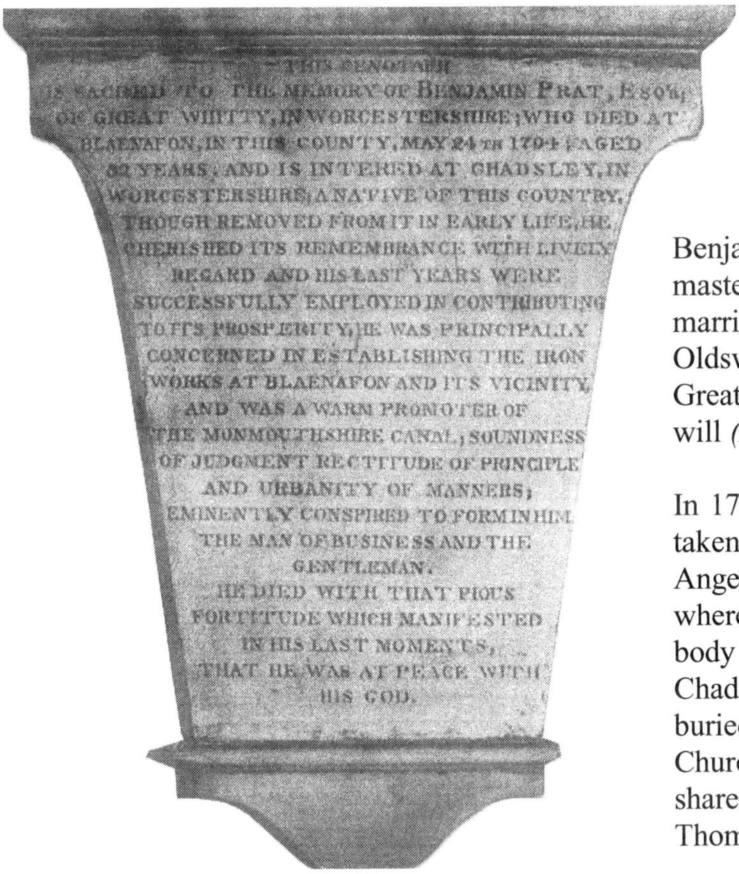

The tablet, dedicated to the memory of Benjamin Pratt, can be found in the nave of St. Woolos Cathedral, Newport.

Benjamin Pratt was an iron master in the Black Country. He married Jane Iddins, in 1767, at Oldswinford, and was living at Great Witley when he made his will *(PRO Prob 11/1249)* in 1788.

In 1794, at the age of 52, he was taken ill, whilst dinning at the Angel Hotel in Abergavenny, where he collapsed and died. His body was brought back to Chaddesley Corbett, where he is buried in St. Cassian's Churchyard with his relations. His share in the ironworks passed to Thomas Hill.

His will, left to his "much esteemed friend Thomas Hill". He made provision for his wife Jane, also leaving to his brother James, mentioned below, and an annuity of ten guineas to his sister Jane. Thomas Hill was his trustee and sole Executor.

The box tomb of Benjamin Pratt, in Chaddesley Corbett Churchyard, who it appears, from the stone tablet above, was originally from Wales.

The Pratt family, lived at Bellington near Barnett Hill, also at Sion House and Dunclent, and worshipped at Chaddesley Corbett Church[1], where in 1812, James Pratt was one of the trustees, who provided three Charity Houses for the poor of the village.

The Charity Cottages in Chaddesley Corbett.

Blaenavon prospered during the French Revolution and the Napoleonic wars, and two further furnaces were built in 1810, together with an additional engine house, to house the steam engine required to provide the additional blast for the new furnaces. This increased the production to over 10,000 tons per year.

Women and children were employed at the ironworks, working a 72-hour week, along side the men, preparing the raw material by breaking the stone into smaller pieces, ready for feeding into the furnaces. Children would gather the material, loading it into wheelbarrows ready for the furnace, and some children, of ten years and upwards were working in the casting houses.

In 1805, Thomas Hill and his nephew Samuel Hopkins, built the church of St. Peter's[2], Blaenavon. It has a number of unusual features, including, cast iron window and door frames, a cast iron font, which is reputed to be the only one of its type in the country, and some of the graves have cast iron covers, all were made at the ironworks. Later, a gallery or balcony was added, supported on cast iron pillars, which makes the interior look more like a chapel than a church.

---

[1] Map Ref SO 891 736
[2] Map Ref SO 251 087

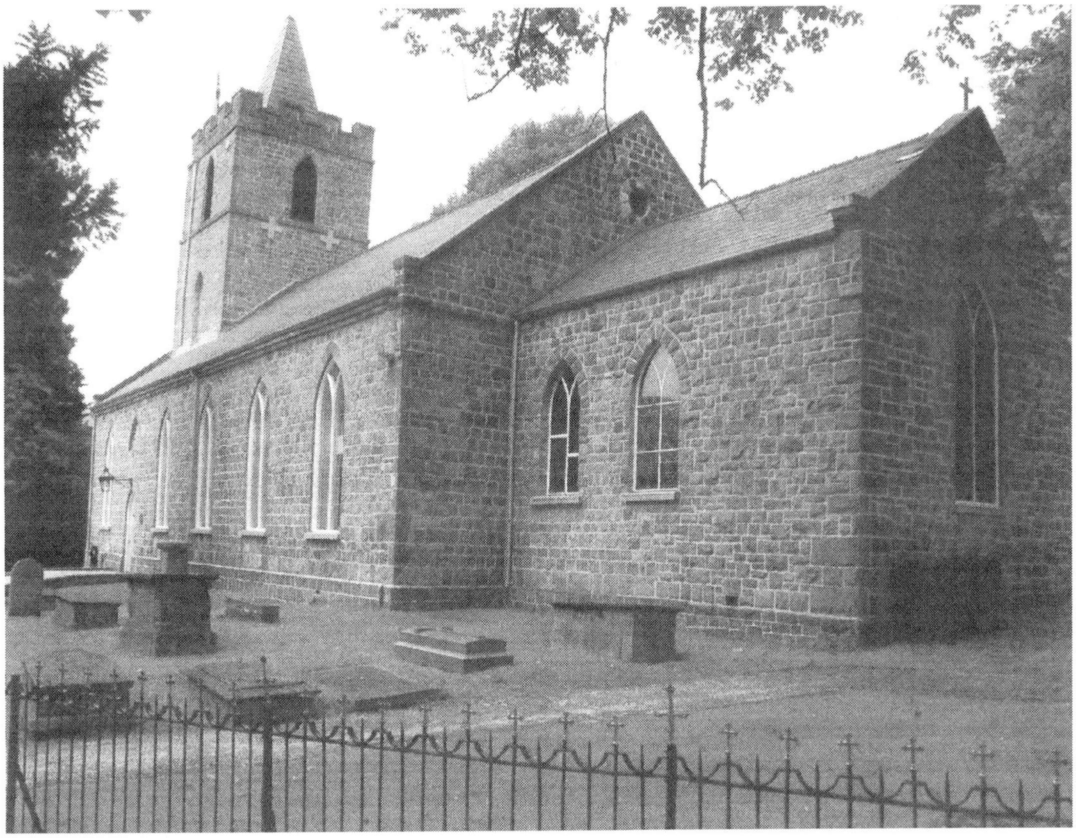

Saint Peter's Church at Blaenavon and the cast iron font shown below.

Eight years later, Thomas Hill decided to build Lye Church, which is said to be facsimile of St. Peter's and probably had a spire similar to above, that was said by the Rev. Dr. Robertson, to have been made of timber[1] and had fallen down "due to old age", which was more likely to have been due to decay.

Transporting the pig iron to the nearest canal, involved the use of packhorses or mules, consisting of dozens of animals in a convoy or train, in charge of drovers. This proved to be an inefficient method of transport, so in 1817, Thomas Hill decided to build a tram road over the mountains to the Brecon and Abergavenny Canal. The route chosen was four miles long, and in some places cut into the side of the hills, with a steep drop on the open side, it also went through a tunnel, over a mile in length, and involved a number of inclines down steep slopes, finally terminating at Llanfoist Wharf, where the Hills had a warehouse, where the iron could be unloaded and stored, or loaded directly onto canal boats and shipped to Newport. The wooden trams, with iron wheels, ran on an angle iron track and were horse drawn, except on the inclines, where mechanical methods were employed. On the return journey, the empty trams were filled with raw materials, and taken back to the Blaenavon ironworks.

[1] It is also thought that the spire might have been covered in shingles, made from riven (split) oak.

Cast iron is limited in its use, since it is brittle and easily broken, it is necessary for it to receive further processing to produce a better quality iron, known as wrought iron, this is usually done in a forge.

Since wrought iron was more profitable than pig iron, the Hills decided that a forge would be an asset, so they built Garnddyrys Forge and also a rolling mill, complete with living accommodation, on the route of their tramway, up in the hills at an altitude of 400m (1300 ft), for the purpose of producing wrought iron.

The process, of converting the pig iron to wrought iron, is called 'puddling', it is done in the forge, and requires the cast iron to be reheated in a special type of furnace, invented by Henry Cort, into a semi solid lump of iron, weighing about 50kg, (one hundred weight) called a bloom. The process is controlled by the puddler, who heats the bloom until the iron reaches the required temperature, it is then pounded with hammers to remove impurities. The Puddlers or Bloomers, as they were sometimes called, were highly skilled and the best paid of the iron workers, they were said to be the aristocrats of the industry, but they often went blind, caused by continually staring at the heated iron, and their lives were shortened by their drinking habits, usually dying before the age of forty.
In this semi solid state, the iron could be passed into the rolling mill and rolled into rails, bars, strips or rods, by passing the bar through a series of grooved rollers, mounted in pairs, which squeezed the red-hot bar to the required shape and size.

To produce one ton of pig iron, it requires three tons of ironstone, two and a half tons of coal, (coke) and one ton of limestone.
And to produce one ton of wrought iron, it requires one and a half tons of pig iron.

Working in the ironworks at this time was most arduous, dirty and fraught with danger, many accidents occurring whilst handling the white-hot liquid iron, often caused by 'splashes', which would immediately burn through normal clothing, causing serious burns. Protective clothing, eye protection, safety boots etc., were unknown. Furnace explosions and sudden splitting of the furnace brickwork, were further hazards, and not uncommon, which would cause a sudden blast or shower of molten iron, like volcanic larva, over the working area of the casting house.

In 1851 there were about 300 people living and employed at Garnddyrys, it is now completely cleared. The iron rails, on which Hills Trams ran, have been removed leaving the ledge, which was cut into the side of the hill, as a footpath, to be enjoyed by walkers. The hills and valleys are free from the grime, smoke, noise and the red glow from the furnaces that lit up the night sky.

Blaenavon ironworks, is the best surviving example of a late eighteenth century ironworks in Great Britain today.

Plaque on St. Peter's Church dedicated to Thomas Hill and his partners.

Thomas Hill was the founder of Lye Church[1], which he built in 1813, at a cost of approximately £9,000. Mr. Hill rented his own pew at the church, and also built a school converted from a stable. In all he provided 14 schools, for the education of poor children of the locality and other districts. He was well liked in Lye, often being referred to as 'Squire' Hill, and many people Christened their children Squire, as a mark of their respect, that they had for him.

His uncle, also called Thomas Hill, left £130 for the education of 20 poor children, of Lye Waste and Careless Green. The first school built at Waste Bank, was built with bricks from the Fimbrel Glasshouse, Amblecote, owned originally by Humphrey Batchelor, which had stood idle for 60 years, and had become derelict. It was dismantled, and the bricks transported to the bottom of Waste Bank, where they were then carried on the heads of the local inhabitants, up the hill to the site of the school, because of the poor condition of the roads. The school was often called Mrs. Batchelor's, school, after Elizabeth Hill.

Lye Church with its second steeple, built in 1880, but became unstable, and was removed in 1980.

The site of Lye Church, had previously been used as the village green, where the popular pursuits of the time had been practiced, including, bare fist fighting, dog fighting, bull baiting, to mention only a few.

The church was built with bricks made on site, from clay excavated on site.

The church, originally built as a Chapel of Ease, which basically was an annex to Oldswinford Church, and as such, had limited powers, and was still in the Parish of Oldswinford.

The presence of the Church and its clergy, had a sobering effect on the mainly nail making community of Lye, who were known to be rough, uncouth, uncivilized and heavy drinkers.

[1] Map Ref SO 923 844

Thomas Hill died in 1824, a very successful gentleman, his will *(PRO Prob 11/1700)* was proved 2nd June 1825. By today's standards, he was a millionaire many times over, and the amounts of money and property he left then, were quite significant, even by today's standards.

He bequeathed to his sons, Thomas and Waldron and grandson Thomas, who were trustees and Executors to his will, all his "messuages farms lands tenements and hereditaments where ever they maybe".

His "Mansion House called Dennis" and the park in which it stood, he left to his son Thomas, also to his son Thomas he left his "Coal and Ironhouse Mills", near Brockmoor, together with Copyhold messuages, lands, tenements and hereditaments, in the Manors of Chaddesley Corbett, Clent and Kingswinford.

Thirteen thousand pounds upon trust for his son Melsup, for his maintenance and care.

Fifteen thousands pounds upon trust for his daughter Mary.

Five thousand pounds upon trust for his daughter Eliza Ann, wife of John Amphlett.

Nothing to his two sons Rev. Henry William and his wife, Susannah Brettell and Rev. Charles and his wife Ann Pyndar, as he had previously made settlements upon them, of twenty thousand pounds.

He bequeathed, a further eleven thousand pounds to his son Thomas.

He mentions his several farms and lands in Oldswinford, and also in Rushock. Messuages, mill, lands and hereditaments in Kingswinford and Wombourne.

He continues, and mentions his capital messuage[1], with the farms and land adjoining in the parish of Broome, now in possession of his son Waldron, and also his capital messuage or Mansion House, called Wollaston Hall with its gardens etc., and his mill and ironworks called Wollaston Mill, "and my several dwellings glasshouses farm lands tenements and hereditaments in Wollaston and Amblecote", all monies and stock etc., he leaves to his sons Thomas and Waldron.

He left twenty thousand pounds, as a marriage settlement, to his son Waldron and his wife Harriet Stephens, to provide for them and their home.

A Codicil, made after completing his will, left further amounts of one thousand pounds[2] each, in addition to the sums previously mentioned, to his sons Melsup, Rev. Charles and Rev. Henry William, Mary and Eliza Ann, his daughters, and four thousand pounds to his son Waldron, charged upon Garnddyrys Forge[3], and to his grandson John Amphlett, he left one hundred pounds.

His will was lengthy, written on ten sheets of paper and the Codicil on two.
He makes no specific mention of his ironworks at Blaenavon.

---

[1] Known as Broome House, where his son Thomas was living before moving to Blaenavon.
[2] One thousand pounds in 1825, would be roughly equal to one million pounds today.
[3] Garnddyrys forge, was part of his iron works at Blaenavon.

The first curate at Lye, was the Rev. Matthew Booker, who died in 1817; he was followed by the Rev. John Hodgson.

The first Incumbent was the Rev. Henry Thomas Hill, the Grandson, of Thomas Hill, the founder of the Church.

Lye Church was dedicated as Christ Church in 1839, splitting Lye from Oldswinford, to form the Parish of Lye.

The appointment of the Rev. Henry Thomas Hill, above, in 1839, may have been brought about by a civil court action, over the ownership of the mining rights to the valuable clay, which lay beneath the Church. This dispute arose between the Rev. Hodgson, the Curate, and the Grandchildren of Mr. Thomas Hill. A newspaper report of the Court proceedings is shown below.

Supplement to the Berrows Worcester Journal – Thursday, March 15, 1838

DOE, ON THE DEMISE OF HILL AND OTHERS v HODGSON
Mr. Sergeant Talfourd (with whom was Mr. Whateley) stated that Mr. Hill, a very benevolent gentleman, feeling that a chapel was much wanted in Old Swinford, he, in the year 1812, built a chapel and a parsonage house there, and Mr. Hill, being a member of the Church of England, wished the Chapel to be put under ecclesiastical authorities, but he had unfortunately died before the arrangements could be completed. Down to the year 1817 Mr. Booker, a clergyman of the Church of England, had officiated, and at his death the present defendant, who was also a clergyman, was put into possession of the parsonage house, and from that time had officiated in the Chapel. Since that time a valuable mine of Stourbridge China-pot clay had been discovered on the premises, and the defendant now claimed the whole property as his own, and insisted on holding it against the heirs of Mr. Hill, who were the present claimants of the property, which was worth about 15,000*l*[1]. The ground of the defendants' claim to the property was that he had been in possession for more than 20 years, but this would really give him no more title than a dissenting minister would have in the Chapel after he was dismissed by the trustees. It was the intention of the present Mr. Hill to endow the Chapel in the way that was intended by his Grandfather, but to reserve to himself the mines, which were under the property.

Mr. Brookes – I live at Lye Waste. I formerly rented the site of the Lye Chapel and parsonage house off Mr. Hill, of Dennis. I gave up part of my taking, about 4 acres, for the buildings &c. The Chapel was built in 1812. The first Minister was Mr. Booker; he lived in the parsonage house. There were about 25 acres more of land, for which I afterwards paid rent to Mr. Booker, by the direction of the late Mr. Hill.

---

[1] In present day values this would probably be worth approximately Fourteen Million pounds, based upon a weekly wage of 10/- per week in 1838, and a gross average wage of £465 per week today in 2004.

Cross-examined by Mr. Sergeant Ludlow – Mr.Booker died in 1817, Mr. Hill in 1824, Mr. Booker was a clergyman. The Chapel is in the parish of Old Swinford. Mr. Foley is the clergyman of Old Swinford. The Chapel in respects conducted as a Chapel of the Church of England, and has an altar, bells, a pulpit, and reading desk, and the sacraments are administered there. The defendant has laid out a considerable sum in improvements.

Mr. Samuel Ebers – I was agent of the late Mr. Hill. I was so from 1805, to his death in 1824. I received rent for the place in question before the Chapel was built. The Chapel and house were built at the expenses of Mr. Hill. Mr. Booker was appointed minister by Mr.Hill, and Divine service has been conducted in the Chapel according to the rites of the Church of England. The late Mr. Hill, expressed an intention to give the land to the Chapel, reserving the mines. About a year ago the defendant said the property was his on account of the length of time he had been in possession. The present claimant, Mr. Hill is the Grandson of my late employer Mr. Hill, who had a key to the Chapel.

Cross-examined – Mr. Hill paid rent to Mr. Booker, and afterwards to the defendant for a pew in the Chapel, and also for a schoolroom, which had been altered from a stable at Mr. Hill's expenses. Mr. Hill had fourteen schools conducted at his own expense, and this was one of them.

Mr. Fiddian – I am the school-master at the Lye Chapel, in January 1837, as I came out of the Chapel, the defendant told me there was a good mine under the property, and that it was as good freehold as any he had, and (if I rightly understood him) he added that he had got [it] in black and white.
Mr. Scott – I was the clerk to Mr. Robins, who was the solicitor of Mr. Hill. After the death of Mr. Robins I examined his papers, but did not find any endowment of the Chapel. I found some drafts of deed on the subject but none executed.

Henry Clifton, Esq. – I am secretary of the Bishops of Worcester. I have attended the visitations for 33 years. The name of the Lye Chapel is not called over as being subject to the bishop's visitation. Mr. Booker said to me, "I don't know how it is that my name is not called over. I don't consider myself within the pale of the church, as I am not called over." I said we did not consider the Lye Chapel as part of the diocese. After that the defendant, who came in canonicals, asked why his name was not called over, and I said to him that, as the Lye Chapel was not consecrated, he ought not to be called.

Cross-examined – both these reverend gentlemen were invited to dine with the bishop and the archdeacon, and were received with the greatest courtesy; but, as this Chapel was not one of those called over, no episcopal letters or citations to visitations were ever sent to the ministers of it. The defendant was formerly curate of Dudley.

Mr. Clowes, proved that he had searched at the Enrolment Office for the endowment of Lye Chapel, but could not find any such endowment, and a demand of the possession of the Chapel was admitted.

Mr. Sergeant Ludlow (with whom was Mr. Richards) said that the defendant's case was brought forward under rather painful circumstances. The defendant had held the curacy of Dudley, and he was introduced by Mr. Hill into this other cure upon the terms of only leaving it with the termination of his life. It had been said that no deed of endowment had been enrolled, but it was clear that, as between man and man, the defendant was appointed to his cure as Mr. Booker was and yet it was thought to turn him out of it without even the ceremony of notice to quit. For the plaintiffs no deeds were produced; the evidence was merely the receipt of rent. Now if that was evidence to show Mr. Hill's title, there was equal evidence of the same kind in favour of the defendant's title, with the additional fact the Mr. Hill had even paid rent to the defendant. It was said that this was like the case of the dissenting Chapel, and that dissenting ministers were liable to be displaced by the Trustees at a moment's warning. That, however, must be taken with some limitation, as in some cases dissenting ministers held their situations for life, and in other cases only during the pleasure of the donors; but that always varied with the terms of the foundation in each particular instance. In the present case there was every presumption, from the way in which both the defendant and his predecessor were placed at this Chapel, and also from all the circumstances, that this Chapel was properly endowed, and that the defendant was appointed to it as a permanent interest. The defendant had laid out a considerable sum at this place, and the plaintiffs had lain by till he had done so, and then sort to turn him out of possession without even offering to repay him the amount of his outlay, a thing they would be bound to do if they had given a mere parole licence to a person to put up any building on their land. Evidence had been given that the defendant had claimed this property as his own freehold, as if he had claimed it for himself and his heirs; but that was not the true construction of what he had said, as all his meant was, that he considered it to be for his life, unless he was guilty of some misconduct.

Mr. Baron Gurney said that it clear that the house and Chapel were built by Mr. Hill, who intended to endow the Chapel, and to reserve the mines. There was no proof that Mr. Hill had made any regular endowment of this Chapel; indeed there was every presumption that he had not. It was competent to persons, with the consent of the clergyman of the parish and the bishop of the diocese, to build and to permanently endow Chapels; but here the evidence was that the defendant had been merely let into possession, without any legal title vested in him. The only question was whether, for more that 20 years the defendant had held this house and Chapel except by the permission of the late Mr. Hill. The defendant's possession was clearly to be referred to the this permission till within this year or two; and then the defendant had claimed the property as his own, and in some degree challenged the plaintiffs to a title. – Verdict for the plaintiffs.

The will of Thomas Hill of Dennis, who died 1824, before the above case was brought to court, made no mention of the clay beneath the Church, or of any property in Lye, and from the proceedings above, it was not produced in court as evidence to what his intentions were, or who he left it to.

The question now arises as to if the result of the above, led to the mining of the clay beneath the Church, which in turn may have caused subsidence, resulting in the steeple becoming unsafe, necessitating its removal in the 1980s?

The Church was consecrated 30th August 1839.

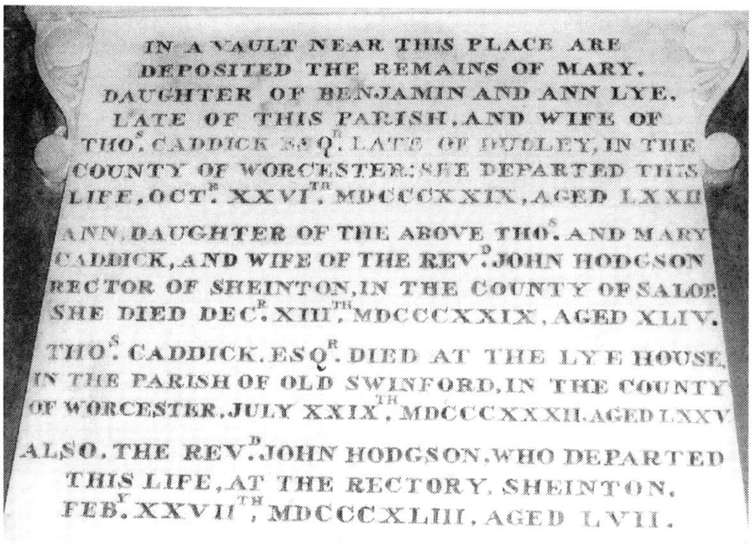

The marble tablet, dedicated to the Caddick family, and also the Rev. John Hodgson, can be found at Enville Church.

The Rev. John Hodgson held the Curacy at Lye, for twenty-two years, previous to that, he had a Curacy at St. Thomas's Church Dudley, from 1810 to 1817, where he married Ann Caddick, 2nd June 1814, daughter of Thomas and Mary Caddick, the officiating clergyman was the Rev. L Booker[1], Vicar. Ann Caddick was baptised at St. Thomas's Church, 29th August 1784.

John was introduced into the Curacy at Lye, in 1817, by Thomas Hill of Dennis.

The records of St. Thomas's Church show a baptism of Mary Ann, daughter of John and Ann Hodgson – Lye House – Minister – by L Booker, 29th November 1821. With the following note *(born 22nd November 1821 – baptised 29th November 1821.)*

On a recent visit to St. Mary's Church, at Enville[2], the above marble tablet, dedicated to the Caddick family was discovered, which shows that John Hodgson was the Rector of Sheinton[3] in Shropshire, where he died 27th February 1843, aged 57. His father-in-law, a retired Timber Merchant of Dudley, died 29th July 1832, aged 75, at his home called 'Lye House', Oldswinford, better known as 'Porridge Hall', Pedmore Road, Lye, or 91 Pedmore Road in more recent times. The Rev. John Hodgson is buried in the Caddick family vault, with his wife Ann and her parents.

Lye House, was once the home of Francis Witton, and was used by Protestant Dissenters as a meetinghouse in 1697. It is also marked on Bache's map of 1699.

William Scott refers to Lye House, in his book 'Stourbridge and its Vicinity' (1832) *"The name of Witton, of Lye is still held in great and deserved respect. Their place of abode, now in no wise distinguished from the line of buildings bordering the road to Wollescot, once stood single and conspicuous. Two venerable yews marked the entrance".*

John Hodgson made his will *(PRO Prob 11/1979)* 12th October 1832, whilst living at Lye House; it was proved and granted to Mary Ann Hodgson, his daughter 24th May 1843. He named his father, James Hodgson as trustee, leaving in trust one-third of

---

[1] The Rev. Doctor Luke Booker, Doctor of Laws and Vicar of Dudley, was the son of the Rev. Matthew Booker of Lye Church 1813-1817.
[2] Map Ref SO 824 868
[3] Map Ref SO 611 040

his estate to his second wife Elizabeth and her children, and the remaining two-thirds in trust for his daughter Mary Ann. There is no reference to the Parish of Sheinton. John's father, James, and one other of the trustees pre-deceased him, leaving two remaining trustees to administer his will.

The Church of Saint Peter and Saint Paul at Sheinton.

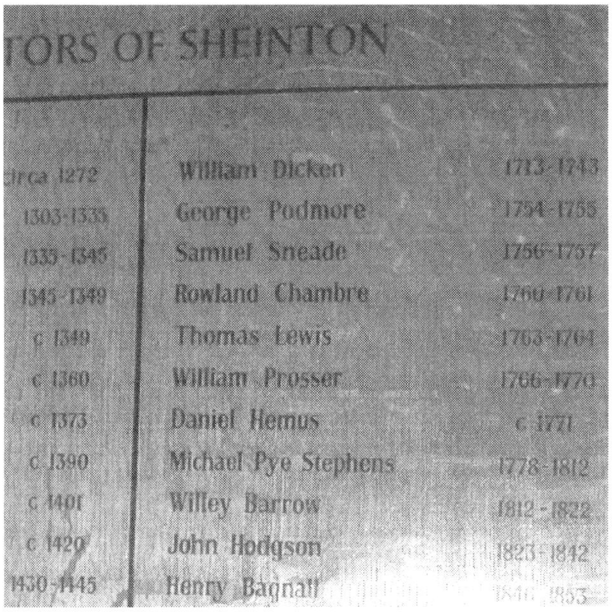

The board showing the Rectors of Sheinton, including John Hodgson 1823-1842.

A visit to the Church of St. Peter and St. Paul in the parish of Sheinton, revealed that John was the Rector there from 1823 to 1842, a period of 19 years, overlapping his service in Lye (1817 to 1839), by 16 years, which seems to be impossible, to be the Rector/Curate at two different churches for 16 years, with a distance of 27 miles between them! This has to be the case of the 'Absent Rector'[1], where he was Rector for the time stated, but the parish was served by a Curate in his absences, who might have been paid by the Rector. Churches often show records of previous Rectors, but rarely show the records of previous Curates.

[1] A similar situation existed at Hadzor, where the Rev. Richard Holmden Amphlett, was the Rector, and the Rev. Reginald Pyndar, was the Curate.

SACRED TO THE MEMORY OF
ANNE
THE BELOVED WIFE OF THOMAS HILL ESQ
OF DENNIS IN THE COUNTY OF STAFFORD;
WHO DIED VII DEC MDCCCX.
AGED LXIX
HER PIETY, CHARITY, AND HUMILITY,
NOTHING COULD EXCEED
HER WHOLE LIFE WAS AN EXEMPLIFICATION
OF THE PRECEPTS OF THE GOSPEL
AND HER CONJUGAL AFFECTION AND MATERNAL CARE
WILL NEVER BE FORGOTTEN
BY THOSE WHO FOUND IN THEM
THEIR GREATEST HAPPINESS.
THIS MEMMORIAL OF HER VIRTURES
WAS ERECTED BY HER AFFECTIONATE HUSBAND.
A.D. MDCCCXI.

BLESSED ARE THE PURE IN HEART,
FOR THEY SHALL SEE GOD.
V. MAT, VIII. VER.

Anne Melsup, wife of Thomas Hill, died 7th December 1810, and is buried at St. Mary's Churchyard, Oldswinford.

Thomas died at Blaenavon in 1824, aged 87. He was brought back to Oldswinford, where he is buried with his wife Anne.

There are two marble tablets, on the north wall of St. Mary's Church dedicated to the memory of Thomas and Anne Hill.

The Hill family are commemorated by a stained glass window in the east wall of Lye Church.

SACRED
TO THE MEMORY OF
THOMAS HILL. ESQ
OF DENNIS
IN THE COUNTY OF STAFFORD,
TO THE MOST ACTIVE BENEVOLENCE
OF DISPOSITION
HE UNITED
THE MOST UNWEARED EXERTION
OF MIND AND BODY
AND AFTER DEVOTING A LARGE PORTION
OF HIS TIME AND FORTUNE
BOTH TO THE TEMPORAL AND ETERNAL
INTERESTS
OF HIS FELLOW CREATURES
DEPARTED THIS LIFE. XVII SEPT
MDCCCXXIV.
AGED LXXXVII

The stained glass window on the east side of Lye Church, dedicated to the Hill family.

The inscriptions beneath each section of the window are:

Left hand side

To the Glory of God and in Thankful Remembrance
Of Thomas Hill of Dennis Park
Founder of this Church

Centre

and of his Grandson
Henry Thomas Hill Prebendary
of Hereford Cathedral the First Incumbent

Right hand side

This Window is Offered by
Relations and Friends
1885

In the 'Heraldry of Worcestershire', by H. Sydney Grazebrook, describes, HILL of Dennis Park near Stourbridge as borne by Thomas Hill (then of Broome) High Sheriff in 1796. Son of Waldron Hill of the "Tiled House" in the County of Stafford – descendent of a respectable family resident at Oldnall near Stourbridge for several generations, died 17th September 1824 aged 87, leaving issue of an eldest son, Thomas[1], who died in 1827.

Melsup Hill of Dennis (1773-1824)

Thomas Hill, throughout his will, seemed most concerned for the welfare of his son Melsup, who it appears, was either an invalid, or had some form of disability. Melsup, aged 51, and unmarried, died shortly after his father, his will *(PRO Prob 11/1695)* was proved 3rd February 1825.

His will was brief and on one sheet of paper only. He refers to owning property to the value of eight thousand pounds plus, held for him by his father. He left £100 to his father, £50 to his brother Thomas, £25 to his brother Waldron, £400 to his brother Charles, £2000 to his sister Eliza Ann, £2000 to his sister Mary, the rest to be put in trust for his brother Henry's children, with his sister Mary as trustee. All other effects to be disposed of and the money arising, to go into trust for his sister Mary. Mary was also the sole Executor. He also added, that any property that should be left to him, by his father, was to go to his sister Mary.

Sarah (Hill) Hopkins of Rugeley

Sarah Hill, sister to Thomas Hill of Dennis, married Thomas Hopkins of Rugeley, owner of a forge at Cannock Wood, known as 'Cankwood'. They had two children, Samuel and Sarah. Thomas Hopkins, previously a iron master, joined Thomas Hill and Benjamin Pratt as a third partner in their South Wales venture, as works manager. He died in 1789, and was replaced by his son Samuel.

Samuel Hopkins of Blaenavon (1762-1815)

Samuel Hopkins was the son of Sarah Hill and Thomas Hopkins, he was baptised in 1762 at Rugeley. He was also the nephew of Thomas Hill of Dennis. He received his father's share of the Blaenavon Ironworks, on his death, and became a managing partner. About 1800, he built himself a house called Ty Mawr (The Big House), known as Blaenavon House, which was later used as a hospital. Samuel Hopkins was 18 years managing partner in the ironworks, and was considered to be a model iron master, distinguished for his benevolence and piety. He attended the English service each Sunday morning at the Church he built with his uncle Thomas of Dennis, and also the Welsh service in the afternoon, although he knew very little Welsh. "Mr. Hopkins" was well liked and respected by his workmen and towns-people; he died in 1815, and is buried in St. Peter's Churchyard amongst his workers.

The will *(PRO Prob 11/1571)* of Samuel Hopkins, made 18th April 1813, left his quarter share in the ironworks to his cousin, Thomas Hill of Broome, now living at Prestwood, giving the Hill family total control.

---

[1] There were four other sons and two daughters, see the family tree inside front cover.

The marble tablet dedicated to Samuel Hopkins can be found in Blaenavon Church.

He appointed his sister Sarah as Executrix and Thomas Hill as Executor to his will, leaving thirty-three thousand pounds in trust to his Trustee, Thomas Hill, his cousin.

The trust, and the income there from, was to be used for the payment of annuities, legacies and various bequests, which he made to a number of people and charities, including his sister, to who, he left an annuity of £2500 per year. To his friend, Doctor William Steel, he left his house in Abergavenny, and an annuity of £250 per year, for the term of his natural life, with legacies of £100 to the infirmary at Stafford, £100 to the sick club of Blaenavon, and £100 to an infirmary at Bangor in Wales.

Sarah Hopkins of Rugeley (1768-1844)

Sarah Hopkins baptised 1768 at Rugeley, niece of Thomas Hill of Dennis, built the school next to St. Peter's Church, Blaenavon, in 1816, in memory of Samuel her brother, it was the first purpose built school in Wales, for the benefit of workers children. The Latin inscription on the front of the school reads "That she may elicit the perpetual praises of God from the mouth of children and that she might in some measure even when he is dead carry into effect the benevolent intentions of her much lamented, great beloved and most deserving Brother, towards her own dear Blaenavonians".
The school operated on The National School System, introduced in 1811, where elder children taught the younger children under the guidance of the schoolmistress or schoolmaster.

Sarah took an active interest in the school, visiting, and following its progress, providing and presenting the school prizes every year, which always consisted of clothing or foot wear. Her last visit was in 1841.
A further school was added in 1860, and a service of commemoration was held at the Church, with the sermon being given by the Rev. Henry Thomas Hill, Rector of Felton (previously of Lye 1839-1843).

Sarah Hopkins never actually lived at Blaenavon, although a frequent visitor to Ty Mawr, she always returned to Rugeley, to her home called "Stone House" in the village of Slitting Mill, where she remained until her death in 1844. She was buried in the family vault in Rugeley Churchyard, the following inscription appears on the vault "In the vault underneath lie the remains of Miss Sarah Hopkins of Stone House in this parish and daughter of Thomas and Sarah Hopkins, who died 19th March 1844, aged 76 years. Blessed are the dead who die in the Lord for they rest from their labours and their words do follow them". The churchyard has now been cleared and the tomb of Sarah and her parents no longer exists.

Stone House, the home of Sarah Hopkins, as it is today (2007).

Sarah, unmarried, made her will *(PRO Prob 11/2002)* 1st March 1841, on eleven sheets of paper, followed with three codicils on a further five sheets, her will was proved 11th July 1844. She appointed her cousin, The Rev. Charles Hill of Bromsberrow, and Walter Landor as her Executors and Trustees, to administer her will and trusts. She was well remembered in Rugeley, where she left money in trust for a school she established, for twenty-five children aged from two to ten years old, chosen by the Vicar, and also provision for a schoolmistress, with an annual salary of fifteen pounds per annum, out of which, she had to provide the coals for heating the class room. She left money for the endowment of the Almshouses, she had built for four poor women and a house for the schoolmistress, which have now been rebuilt, but still have the stone tablet to her memory, from the original Almshouses. She bequeathed money to additional trusts to increase the size of the local Anglican Churches in order to provide free seating for the local inhabitants, "Which must not be used to provide private pews". She left £100 pounds to the Sick Club of Blaenavon, £100 pounds to the general infirmary of Stafford, £100 pounds to the infirmary at Hereford, £100 to her cousin Mary, spinster, and an annuity of £50, per year, £100 to her cousin the Rev. Edward Hill of Hindley, Lancaster, £50 to her cousin the Rev. Hopkins Hill, plus an annuity of £50 per year. She left the yearly sum of £13, to Benjamin Lewis, a blind man of Coyity, near Blaenavon, to be paid to him at the rate of five shillings weekly, and £20 annuity to her servant Mary Riley, and £10 annuities to her servants Hannah Edwards, and Thomas Collier, and £6 to Lucy Colwick. To John Coldwell, master at the free school at Blaenavon, she left the annual sum of £15, to her Godchildren **Anne Hill** and **Peter Hill**, children of her late cousin Henry Hill, she left £50 each, and to her cousin The Rev. Henry Thomas Hill, eldest son of (The Reverend) Henry (William) Hill, she left £100. To her cousins Emma Katherine Baker, and Caroline Sarah Baker she left £50 each.

The school, for 25 children, founded by Sarah Hopkins, and endowed by her, was originally a cottage, shown above on the left, of which only part remains, and is now part of the Church on the right, which is 'The Church of St. John the Baptist'. The white house is built on part of the foundations of the former school; Sarah called it "Cannock Chase Cottage School".

The above Almshouses are the replacements for the original ones. The stone corbels at the eaves, copings and the stone tablet, shown above, were taken from the original Almshouses, the latter being fixed to the large gable on the left, which reads "These Almshouses for four poor women and the schoolmistress's house, were erected and endowed by Mrs. Sarah Hopkins of Stone House. AD 1826". ('Mrs.' was a courtesy title often given to unmarried elderly ladies).

Slitting Mill is a village that can be found on the Penkridge Bank Road from Penkridge to Rugeley, named after the water driven slitting mill, which at one time existed near by. It is on the outskirts of Cannock Chase, just before entering Rugeley. Previously it was called 'Stonehouse', after the house occupied Sarah Hopkins.

Stone House[1] was built in 1584 on the site of a quarry, from which the stone was excavated to build the house, with its cellars built into the void left after removing the stone. The house had various owners/occupiers, who added and enlarged the original structure, including Sarah Hopkins who occupied it from 1808, and owned it from 1826, up to her death in 1844. During the Second World War, it was taken over by the War Department and used by the RAF, who added two Nissan huts in the grounds, it was abandoned by the RAF in 1958 and left to the vandals and the elements. It became a grade 2 listed building, situated within the green belt. Soon it became derelict and dangerous. Various developers bought the five-acre site, suggesting various uses, including a clubhouse; offices, flats, houses and bungalows, all were rejected. Finally, after ten years of wrangling, a businessman bought it for his own occupation, who has sympathetically restored and modernised it.

The slitting mill stood an the banks of a stream called 'The Rising Brook', which ran through Cannock Chase and down through Rugely to the River Trent, supporting at least seven water mills on its journey. The slitting mill made rod used by the nailers to forge nails, and was owned by Thomas Hopkins and his son Samuel Hopkins. The previous home, of the Hopkins family, was 'Fair Oaks House', which was near by. Fair Oaks House was later demolished and its site used for houses.

The Sarah Hopkins Trust built the chancel of The Parish Church of St. Agustine of Canterbury, Rugeley, and also provided the oak pulpit, made in 1907, which is dedicated to the memory of Sarah. The carving on the front panel is of Saint Agustine, it is said to contain "a fine amount of detail".

The pulpit and the brass plate dedicating it to Sarah Hopkins, which is fixed to the side.

[1] Map Ref SO 029 177

It was said Sarah was fond of entertaining, and often held parties and dances at Stone House, to which the young ladies and gentlemen of Rugeley were invited.

This seems to be borne out by the 1841 census that shows on the day of the census there were twelve other people, besides Sarah staying in her house. Two were her cousins, Emma Baker and Caroline Baker, who were the grandchildren of her aunt Mary, who married William Waldron, and mentioned in her will. Four were her servants, and the rest were presumably, her guests.

The Stone House sign at the main entrance, with Stone House in the background.

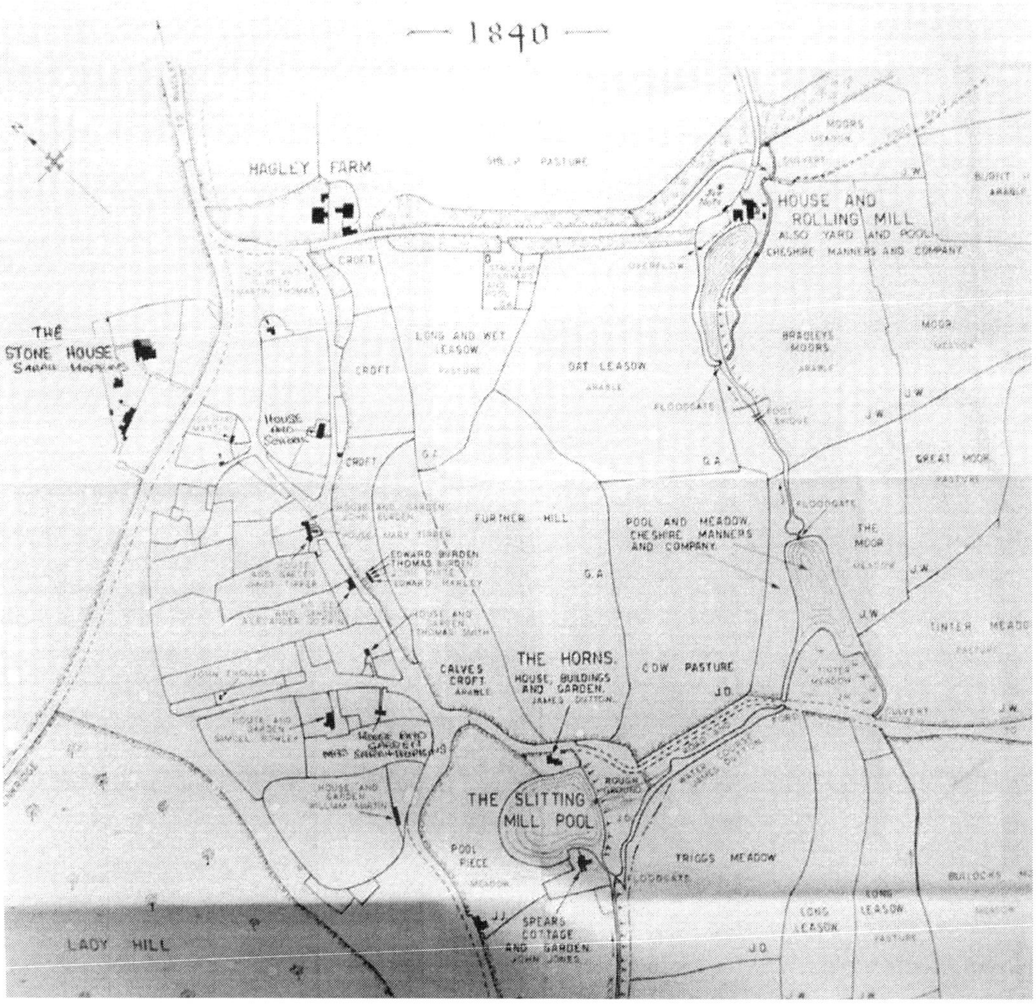

The map of the village of Slitting Mill in 1840, showing the Stone House towards the top left, with the School just to its right, and slightly lower, by the two crofts. A second house, belonging to Mrs. Sarah Hopkins, is shown towards the bottom left, almost on a line with the slitting mill pool.

The Slitting Mill dates back to 1623, and is probably the slitting mill, listed as part of the group of ironworks owned by "The Staffordshire Works", in the 17th century, of which the Foley's were partners, and included 'a slitting mill at Rugeley and a forge at Cannock', the slitting mill is easy to identify, whereas, the site of the forge is more difficult to pin point.
"The Fair Oaks House", previously mentioned, was also called "The Forge", and owned by Thomas Hopkins, who referred to it as "Cankwood" in his will. Cank is the name of the river god, a figure made of lead, and known as 'Old Cank', who sat on a bridge overlooking the Rising Brook. Could this be the forge in question?

Rugeley is 'famed' for a number of murders that took place there. The first, in 1839, was the murder of Christina Collins, by three boatmen, on a canal boat, whose mutilated body was found in the canal. The three men were tried at Stafford and found guilty and sentenced to death, one received a last minute reprieve, and the other two were hung at Stafford.

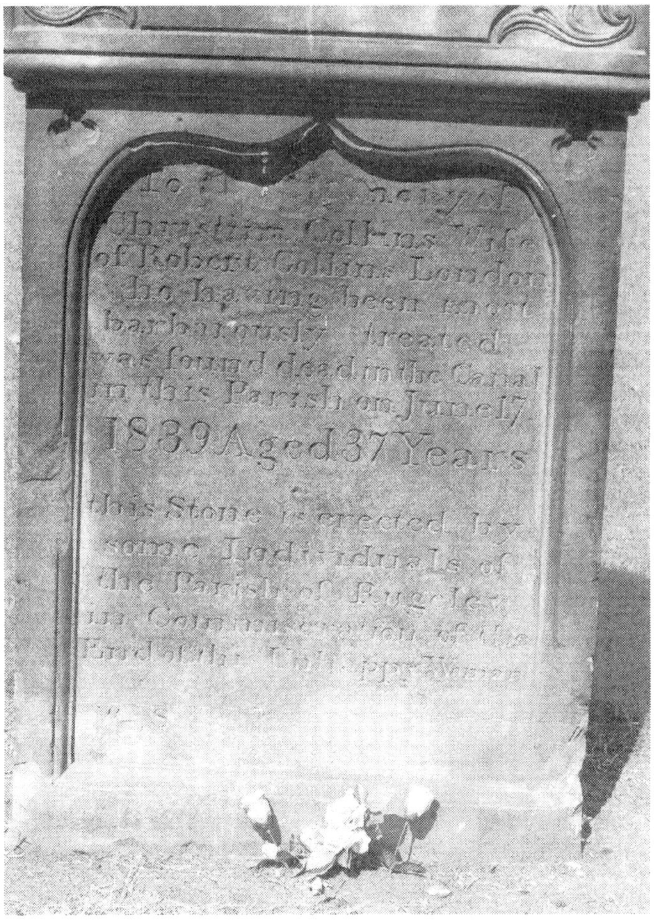

The grave of Christina Collins.

The second murder was more notorious, since it involved a number of deaths. Doctor William Palmer had a general practice in Rugeley in 1855, he also had an uncontrollable gambling habit, from which he sustained huge losses, which his income could not cover, so he developed an ingenious system of making up his losses by insuring the lives of his patients, including his own family, and poisoning them with strychnine, he then signed the death certificate and picked up the insurance money to pay his debts!
He is thought to have killed between ten and fifteen people. All went well until the insurance company started to ask questions. He was not tried at Stafford as it was considered, that a jury consisting of local people might be prejudiced against him! So he was tried at the Old Bailey, London, found guilty and hung at Stafford.

The grave of Christina Collins still exists in the churchyard of Rugeley Parish Church, and also the grave of John Parson Cook, who was a friend and victim of Doctor William Palmer, the "Rugeley Poisoner" in 1855.

Thomas Hill (2) of Broome (1767-1827)

Thomas Hill born 1767 was the son of Thomas Hill of Dennis, he married Anne Lilly and they lived at Broome House (owned by his father), and worshipped at St. Peter's Church, Broome[1], where a number of their children were baptised, privately. Anne, his wife, died the 22nd September 1804, at Broome, aged 35, leaving him with a number of young children. A sculptured marble memorial by Flaxman, dedicated to her memory by Thomas, can be found on the north wall of the Church. The barefooted female figure reading the book is said to be his wife Anne.
Anne was buried in Oldswinford Churchyard on the 29th September, 1804.

Flaxman John, R. A. (1755-1826), a great English sculptor who was born at York, and at twenty was employed as modeller by Wedgewood; showing great ability as a sculptor he went to Italy and studied there seven years. On his return was made an R.A. and Professor of Sculpture, and thenceforward his career was one of unqualified success. *(Pears Cyclopaedia)*

Saint Peter's Church, Broome, its earliest Rector is recorded in 1190.

In 1808, Thomas and his father owned the bank on the corner of Coventry Street and High Street, Stourbridge, known as the Old Bank, and were joined in partnership by William Robins and Thomas Bate, the bank being known as Hill, Bate & Robins.

Thomas Hill of Dennis died aged 87 in 1824, his share in the ironworks passing to his sons Thomas of Broome, Waldron and grandson Thomas.

---

[1] Map Ref SO 902 784

SACRED TO THE MEMORY OF
ANNE
THE BELOVED WIFE OF THOMAS HILL ESQ
OF BROOME IN STAFFORDSHIRE
AND DAUGHTER OF WLLIAM LILLY ESQ OF WORCESTER
POSSESSING AN AMIABLE DISPOSITION, AND
AN AFFECTIONATE HEART
SHE FUFILLED WITH TENDER CARE EVERY,
DOMESTIC AND SOCIAL DUTY,
TO THE HAPPINESS OF HER FAMILY, AND TO THE
BENEFIT OF SOCIETY;
AND HAVING THESE ENDEARING VIRTUES,
FOUNDED ON THE SOLID BASIS OF OUR HOLY RELIGION
WAS PREPARED TO MEET THAT AWFUL SUMMONS
WHICH SUDDENLY CALLED HER TO THE REALMS OF BLISS
SEPTEMBER THE 22ND 1804.
AGED 35 YEARS.

The Flaxman and the inscription to the memory of Anne, wife of Thomas Hill of Broome.

In 1816 Thomas Hill of Broome and his children moved to Blaenavon, to join his father at the ironworks, this move probably being influenced by the death of his cousin Samuel Hopkins in 1815, who left him his quarter share in the ironworks, giving the Hills full control. He continued to take more responsibility from his ageing father, which he shared with his brother Waldron, and his son Thomas, who would now be aged 34.

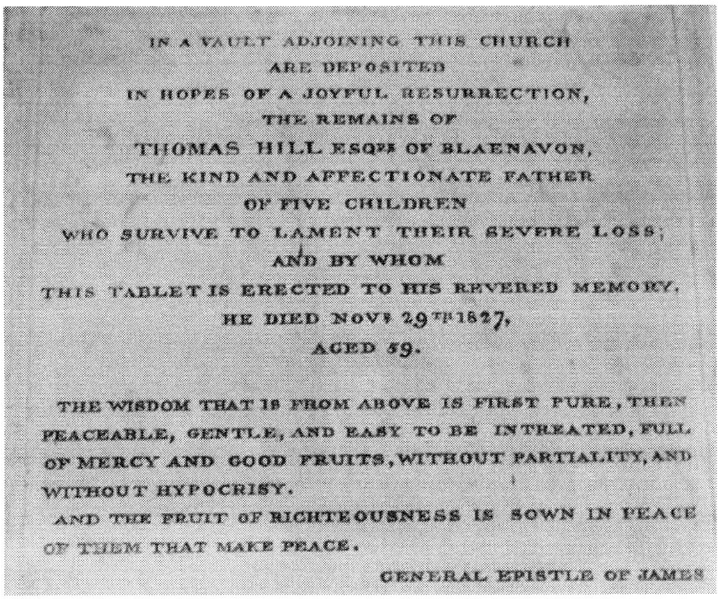

The tablet, erected in Blaenavon Church to Thomas Hill of Broome.

Thomas continued to run the ironworks, but he was not a popular man. He was said to be arrogant and made himself unpopular with his workers. He died in 1827; his life was shortened by his extravagant lifestyle, some of which could have been attributed to the loss of his wife and the depression in the iron trade that followed the end of the Napoleonic war in 1815.

Thomas Hill of Broome, now known as Thomas Hill of Blaenavon, is buried at Blaenavon in the graveyard of St. Peter's Church, where the above tablet, dedicated to him, can be found inside the Church.

It was said that St. Peter's Church at Blaenavon, was built in memory of Anne Lilly, the wife of Thomas, and named after St. Peter's Church at Broome.

The will *(PRO Prob 11/1742)* of Thomas, made 1st April 1824, left everything to his son Thomas Hill, including his share in the Ironworks, the Forge at Garnddyrys and the house, known as Park House, where the Hills lived at Blaenavon, subject to the payment of £6000 each to his four daughters.
He also left to his friend, Miss Eliza Cooke £200 and £110 per year salary, as long as she remained with his daughters.
To Sarah Brazier, he left an annuity of £100 per year for her natural life, plus £10 per year for the board, clothing and education of her son George Brazier, as long as he continued to live with her. With the proviso, that if George Brazier is put to school and brought up under the direction and approbation of his Executors, he directed that he be put out to apprenticeship, to learn a trade or profession, or that the situation of an agent be found for him, and requested the attention of his Executors to the said George Brazier, so that he could be placed in a responsible situation where he can procure a honest livelihood, and directed that all necessary expenses be paid for him until he was able to provide for himself.
He named his son Thomas and Robert Wheeley as Executors, leaving Robert Wheeley £100 for his trouble.
He left instructions, that none of his relatives should wear mourning for more that six months after his decease.

Eliza Ann (Hill) Amphlett of Clent (1770-1837)

Eliza Ann Hill was the daughter of Thomas Hill of Dennis, born 19th September 1770, who married John Amphlett, the Squire of Clent, 17th February 1789. She was a sister to Thomas Hill of Broome. They had nine children including **John**, born 13th September 1795, who continued the Amphlett line, with a further three generations of **John Amphletts**, up to the death of John Amphlett in 1945, when the male line ended.

Eliza Anne died in 1837, aged sixty six years, her G^{2}grandson, **Edward Baylie Amphlett,** Captain and Adjutant in the 12th Worcestershire Regiment, was killed in the Dardanelles 4th June 1915, aged thirty eight.

Probably the best known, was **John Amphlett** 1845 to 1918, the G grandson of Eliza Ann Hill, who wrote the book "A Short History of Clent", he was the seventh Squire of Clent. The history of the Amphlett family reaches back much further than Clent, to Hadzor, near Droitwich, and Ombersley, previous to that. Hadzor is also mentioned later in this book, with regards to another member of the Hill family.

The Amphlett family formally owned the manor of Hadzor, before moving to Clent about 1660. Many of the family are interred in Hadzor Parish Church of St. John the Baptist, including William Amphlett, who is described as a 'Gent, Lord of this Manor', who died 6th June 1662, aged 74.

William Amphlett bought the manor of Hadzor, in 1623 from John Copley. The Amphlett family held it until 1822, when it was sold by the Rev. Richard Holmden Amphlett, who was the Rector, to John Howard Galton, at the same time he bought Wychbold Hall, Dodderhill, where he died in 1842, the Hall passing to his son, The Right Hon. Sir Richard Paul Amphlett, who in the 1881 census, was described as a

'Retired Judge of Supreme Court of Appeal & Privy Council', born at Quatt in 1809, Shropshire, living at 32, Wimpole Street, London.
Sir Richard Paul Amphlett, is also interred in the family vault at Hadzor Church.
There is also a tablet dedicated "To the memory of the Rev. Richard Holmden Amphlett M.A. Rector of this parish, who died 8th March 1842 and his wife Sarah".

There was a previous Richard Amphlett, who also married a Sarah, he was baptised at St. Michael's Bedwardine Church, Worcester, on the 25th September 1687, whose parents were William and Amy. Richard married Sarah Hyatt, 18th February 1714 at Almeley, Hereford, an elaborate tablet in the chancel reads:

Sacred to the memory of Lady Sarah Amphlett, the affectionate wife of Richard Amphlett, Esq., and heiress of Charles Hyatt, of noble birth, of Almeley, in the County of Hereford. She died in peace and faith on the 29th March, 1739, aged 37. Under this same stone, near the remains of his esteemed wife, is interred the body of Richard Amphlett, Esq., truly the patron of this Church a man of irreproachable conscientiousness and strict integrity. Distinguished for his affection towards his friends, his liberality towards the poor, and his kindness towards all. He impartially dispensed justice to all. He promoted the cause of religion not less by his example than by his conversation. He died on the 13th June, 1743, aged 54.

The Amphlett family home, at Hadzor, was a large part timbered Elizabethan house, known as Hadzor House, surrounded by an extensive estate, with the church in the same grounds, being only a few steps away. The House was rebuilt and extended about 1830, by John Howard Galton, who also modified the church about 1835. Some time later the Galton's renamed the House 'Hadzor Hall'.

The Galtons were gun makers in Birmingham, and owned or leased a mill in Hartle Lane, Belbroughton, known as Galtons gun barrel mill.

Thomas Hill (3) of Blaenavon (1790-1868)

Thomas Hill (3) baptised at Broome in 1790, inherited his father's share of the ironworks on his death in 1827. He ran the works in partnership with his uncle Waldron until he retired in 1830; he was then assisted by Robert Wheeley from Stourbridge, as works manager and partner.

Robert Wheeley was brought to Blaenavon by Thomas Hill of Dennis, and married the daughter of James Jenkins, the parson at St. Peter's Church, he died 2nd July 1851, aged 61, he is buried in a tomb in Blaenavon Churchyard.

Thomas Hill (3), the grandson of Thomas of Dennis; was educated at Eton and Oxford. "It was often considered vulgar to be 'in trade', even as a rich industrialist, and third generation business man, who desired to distance himself from industry and was remembered as a typical country squire"[1].

After the death of his grandfather he became a partner in the bank, Hill, Bate and Robins in Stourbridge.

---

[1] Quotation from 'Blaenavon Ironworks' by Jeremy K. Knight BA, FSA

Thomas Hill (3) retired from the bank in 1833, and concentrated on the ironworks, which he attempted to sell at this time, but it failed to reach the reserve price.
In 1836, he sold the company to the Blaenavon Iron and Coal Company for £222,000, this ended the era of ownership by the Hill family. He sold the Dennis Estate by auction in 1838, and retired to Ross, but still had some business relationships at Stourbridge, he died in 1868 at Rudhall.

William Seager Wheeley, brother of Robert Wheeley, bought the Dennis Estate in 1839.

The Blaenavon Ironworks[1] continued producing iron up to about 1904. It later closed and became derelict and in a dangerous condition, demolition was considered, some of the stone having already been salvaged to build the Church of Saint James in the town of Blaenavon. It was saved and put into the care of the Welsh Historic Monuments, who took over its guardianship in 1974, and now has 'World Heritage Site' status, equal to that of 'The Great Wall of China' – 'Hadrian's Wall' – 'The Taj Mahal' – 'Stonehenge' – 'The Grand Canyon' – 'The Great Barrier Reef' and others.

Waldron Hill of Broome and Heavitree (1775-1844)

Waldron Hill married Harriet Stephens about 1794, at Sheinton[2] Parish Church, where her father, the Reverend Michael Pye Stephens, was the Rector from 1778 to 1812. Their eldest son, **Waldron Stephens Hill**, was born at Blaenavon and baptised at Broome, 20th October 1808. There was also a daughter called **Catherine**, baptised in 1809. Their second son, born 1811, was called Hopkins, he was also baptised at Broome. Waldron was living at Broome at the time his father, Thomas Hill of Dennis, made his will on the 29th June 1822. Waldron shared the ironworks with his brother Thomas and his nephew, also called Thomas, which was left them by Thomas Hill of Dennis, and assisted in its running after the death of his brother in 1827. Waldron Hill of Broome, retired from the ironworks in 1830, and died in 1844 at Mount Le Grand, Heavitree, Exeter, Devon, his will, on two sheets of paper, made 28th March 1844, left every thing to his wife Harriet, with the proviso that certain items were to pass to their son Waldron Stephens Hill after the death of Harriet.

Reverend Hopkins Hill (1811-....)

The Rev. Hopkins Hill, was the son of Waldron and Harriet Stevens, he was baptised at Broome on the 14th September 1811, named after his Godfather Samuel Hopkins, of Blaenavon. He was also remembered in the will of Sarah Hopkins. He was the Vicar of Ocle Pychard, Herefordshire, from 1845 to 1869. (See page 61)

Reverend Charles Hill of Bromsberrow (1786-1856)

The Rev. Charles Hill, was the son of Thomas Hill of Dennis, born in 1786. Very little was known about him, except that he was recorded in the Oldswinford records, from May 1815 to October 1816, on five occasions, when he baptised children of his father's servants at St. Mary's Church, Oldswinford.

---

[1] Map Ref SO 247 093

[2] See Sheinton Church and the Rectors Board on page 27.

The will of Thomas Hill of Dennis, mentions Charles as being married to Anne Pyndar, which led to finding his marriage was recorded 19th January 1818, at Areley Kings[1], just outside Stourport. At the time of his wedding he was living at Prestwood House in the Parish of Kinver, another property thought to be owned or leased by his father Thomas Hill.

Saint Bartholomew's Church, at Areley Kings and the Layaman font below.

The Church and the Layaman Font at Areley Kings are of great significance. The font was found beneath the floor of the Nave during rebuilding in 1886. It was originally cut from one piece of stone, but when unearthed was found to be broken into four parts, and built into the rubble wall supporting the floor.
The inscription on the base reads TEMPORE : LAYAMANNI : SANTI 'In the time of Saint Layaman', which refers to the first priest of the Church in the twelfth Century, who was the writer of early verse and the author of 'Brut', who recorded that he 'dwelt in Ernleye at a church beside the Severne.' The fragmented font was rebuilt with a new bowl made of York stone, carved in Hereford and fixed onto the original round column.

[1] Map Ref SO 802 710

Church House, with St. Bartholomew's Church in the background.

The plaque on the side of Church House.

The half timbered building near to the Church, known as Church House, built in 1536, has two meeting rooms for holding celebrations known as 'Ales', it was restored and provided with modern facilities in 2006.

A baptism of a Reginald Pyndar Hill, 28th June 1820 was recorded at Bromsberrow, which is close to the Gloucestershire – Herefordshire border, by Charles and Anne Hill. A second baptism of Reginald Pyndar Hill, took place at Oldswinford on the 31st January 1821.

A second son, William Charles Hill, was baptised at Bromsberrow the 26th May 1831.

A visit to Bromsberrow, near Ledbury, found Charles Hill had been the Rector at St. Mary's Church[1], Bromsberrow from 1823 to 1856, a period of 33 years. He died in 1856 aged 69, and is buried in the Churchyard.

---

[1] Map Ref SO 742 336

The Church of Saint Mary at Bromsberrow above, and its entrance porch below.

The Church, which can be found at the end of a long drive, next to a farm, is a delightful part timbered building, the entrance porch being of timber framed construction. The age of the Church is unknown, but previous Rectors date back to 1280.

Bromsberrow Church of St. Mary, was stone built during the 13th century, the upper part of the tower is timber framed with a shingled[1] spire, which was rebuilt 1875.

The grave of Charles Hill and his wife Anne.

A stained glass window to the memory of the Rev Charles Hill and his wife Anne, can be found on the south wall of the Church, dedicated by their two sons Reginald Pyndar and William Charles.

Part of the stained glass window in memory of Charles Hill and his wife Anne dedicated by their sons.

---

[1] Shingles are a form of wooden roof tile, generally made from red cedar today, but in the past were made from riven oak, oak that has been split to follow the grain.

The village of Bromsberrow is a straggling village, spread out along country lanes. A new rectory is near the bottom of the drive, but the old rectory still survives, which is a considerable distance from the Church, which would have been best reached in the past, by walking across fields and over hills. The population in 1851 was 260. Included in the listed gentry was the Rev. Charles Hill M.A. Rector.

The spire of Saint Michael and all Angels Church, at at the top of Church Lane, Ledbury.

The Rev. Reginald Pyndar, father-in-law of Charles Hill died in 1831, there is a stained glass window to his memory in the Chapter House of Ledbury Church[1].

[1]Map Ref SO 713 377

The Church of St. Michael and all Angels, is very large, almost of Cathedral proportions, if compared with other churches visited, serving the bustling market town of Ledbury.

Anne was the daughter of the Rev. Reginald Pyndar and his wife Mary. What exactly was the role of the Rev. Reginald Pyndar at Ledbury Church is unknown; his name is not recorded on the list of Rectors. Neither is his previous record of service at various other churches, of which there is quite a few.

His marriage to Mary Foxcroft is recorded at Nottingham in 1781. His first Daughter Katherina, was baptised 1st December 1782, at Rochester Staffs.

His will *(PRO Prob 11/1794)* tells us he was formally of Hadzor House in the County of Worcester, near Droitwich, his daughter Anne, was baptised at Hadzor, and so were other members of his family.

Hadzor Church of St. John the Baptist was said to have existed in 1268. It was rebuilt in the mid fourteen century, and modified around 1835. The tower has one bell. It was once the Parish Church of Hadzor, it still exists, but is deconsecrated, and is privately owned, the final service being held 11th April 1971. It is on the estate of Hadzor Hall, the Hall itself being only a few yards away. On the south side of the church, against the chancel wall, there once was an opening, about four feet from the ground, where leprous persons could receive holy communion.

Hadzor Church of St. John the Baptist. Note the lepers opening below the second window from the right. The condition of the Church is poor, both internally and externally and at the moment it serves as a store.

The Rev. William Waldron, M.A., born at Belbroughton in 1670, was the Rector here for 47 years, he married Mary Wheeler, at St. Peter's Church, Droitwich, in 1708, they had two children, both baptised at Hadzor, he died in 1741 aged seventy-one.

In 1770 the Rev. Reginald Pyndar qualified as a Justice of the Peace.
The Quarter Sessions Rolls of 1797, mentions the Rev. Reginald Pyndar, who was at that time living at Himbleton.
He was later mentioned 8th October 1822, at the Quarter Sessions at Gloucester, where Rev. Reginald Pyndar JP, of Upper Hall, Ledbury, tried two men for having a gun. He tried a similar case at Hereford, 2nd September 1823.
In March to July 1826, he was a magistrate at Hereford, where, on one occasion, he awarded a sentence of 3 months hard labour.

Hadzor House, was once the residence of Reginald Pynder, mentioned in his will, which was originally a 16th century half timbered building, on the present site of the now Hadzor Hall, which was rebuilt about 1830. Trying to define exactly when he lived at Hadzor House/Hall is rather difficult, since he is not recorded as owning it, or of having lived there. The only evidence is his will, and the births of three of his children, including Anne, who are recorded there between 1786 and 1796. The only record at this time, is that it was owned by the Rev. Richard Holmden Amphlett, and the only possible theory, is that he was a Rector elsewhere, (his son Sir Richard Paul Amphlett was born at Quatt 1809) and Reginald Pyndar was the Curate at Hadzor in his absence and living in Hadzor House.

He also mentions in his will that he lived at Areley House, in the parish of Areley Regis, and since Charles Hill married his daughter at Areley Kings in 1818, which presumably is the same place, but again after visiting the Church, he is not recorded on the list of Rectors, perhaps again he was only the Curate?
His will made in 1831, continues, stating that he now lives at his mansion house called Upper Hall, Ledbury.

He bequeathed to the Rev. John Turner of Hagley, the sum of £50 "as a mark of my affectionate regards and esteem". John Turner was Rector of St. John the Baptist Church[1] at Hagley 1804 to 1847.

Reginald Pyndar died in 1832, aged 76, his will left every thing in trust, to be divided into six parts to provide for his wife and five daughters, Charles Hill was named as one of his Executors.
He refers to his eldest daughter Katherina, as Lady Sherbrooke, the widow of Sir John Coape Sherbrooke, Knight Grand Cross of the Bath, deceased.

The will of Dame Katherina Coape Sherbrooke, of Calverton, 4th June 1855, left £6000 to her sister Anne Hill, wife of Charles Hill of Bromsberrow.

Hadzor is an interesting village; it is spread out along narrow county lanes, but is rather spoilt by the noise from the M5 motorway nearby. It has a Roman Catholic Chapel of St. Richard and St. Hubert, with a small school attached, situated in Hadzor Wood, which was built by Mr. T. H. Galton of Hadzor Hall, in 1878.

Protestant children of the parish originally went to school at Oddingley, which is the next parish to Hadzor, its Church was said to be an annex to Hadzor Church, and the Rev. Reginald Pyndar would have officiated at both Churches.

---

[1] Map Ref SO 921 808

Saint James Church, Oddingley.

St. James Church, Oddingley[1] is late 15th century; it was restored in 1860, using the original windows and ancient stained glass, it became an annex to Hadzor sharing the same Rector and Protestant School. The Church, in the form of a crucifix, it is small, plain and simple, a real country Church. It is set back from the road, and reached by a track with little or no parking space. There is a memorial tablet to the Rev. Charles Tookey of Belbroughton.

Oddingley is famed for a double murder that took place there in the early 19th century. In 1793 the Rev. George Parker was introduced to the living and received tythes from the local farmers, to the value of £130, which he considered inadequate and wanted to increase them to £150, which the farmers bitterly opposed, and banded together and refused to pay. On the 24th June 1806, he was shot from a nearby field, but managed to stagger towards his assailant, who battered him to death, with the butt of the gun. It was clear that the murderer was a local man, named Richard Hemming, who went into hiding in a barn at Nether Wood Farm, on the road to Crowle, where he was also murdered and his body hidden in the barn, and a story put about that he had gone to America. Twenty-six years later, in 1830, his body was found. Three men were accused of being involved in his murder, and others were also implicated. They were tried at Worcester Assizes, 11th March 1830, and found not guilty on a technicality in the law that existed at that time.

A Bible and Common Prayer book, originally presented to Hadzor Church by Richard Holmden Amphett in 1891, can now be found in St, James's Church, Oddingley.

[1] Map Ref SO 915 591

The village of Hadzor appears to have had quite a Catholic influence, and it is said, that a number of Catholics settled here, many years ago for some reason; this is reflected in the names of many of its half-timbered buildings, which are named after Saints.

Hadzor Court above.

One prominent building in the village is Hadzor Court, built in the 15th century, which also had a Catholic association, in so much, that its present owner, whilst carrying out restoration work, found a number of 'priest holes', intended to hide Catholic Priests who were being persecuted at one time.

The tower and turret of Court Farm.

Hadzor Court and the farm next door to it, was once one building, known as Old Court Farm. The farm, now separate, is called Court Farm, it also is a very interesting building. It has a tower crowned with a timber turret complete with finials, which was probably the original, but is now in a sad state of repair, and is likely to collapse at some time in the near future.

Hadzor Hall rebuilt about 1830 by John Howard Galton and named by him.

The Rev. Reginald Pyndar, was eventually found to be the Rector at Madresfield Church of St. Mary the Virgin[1], Malvern, from 1793 until he died in 1831, a period of thirty-eight years, which suggests 'another case of the absent Rector[2]', where the parish was served by a Curate in his absence. He was also a member of the Pyndar family who owned Madresfield Court, a short distance away.

Madresfield Court was inherited by the Lygon family, who were of Norman descent, who arrived in this country with William the Conqueror.

Margaret Lygon married Reginald Pyndar of Kempley in 1713, their eldest son, Reginald, assumed the name of Lygon, and his son, William, born 1747, became the 1st Earl of Beauchamp, he died in 1816, the Rev. Reginald Pyndar was his cousin.

The Church font was a gift from John Reginald Pyndar, 3rd Earl of Beauchamp in 1852.

Charles Hill, son-in-law to the Rev. Reginald Pyndar, also became the Rector of Madresfield Church, following the death of his father-in-law, where he was Rector from 1832 to 1856; he was also Rector at Bromsberrow from 1823 to 1856, an overlap of 24 years, he died in 1856.
There is a memorial in the churchyard, at the east end of the Church, to Charles Hill.[3]

---

[1] Map Ref SO 804 475
[2] It is said that at certain times over 50% of Incumbents of parish Churches were absentees.
[3] Charles Hill is buried at Bromsberrow Church.

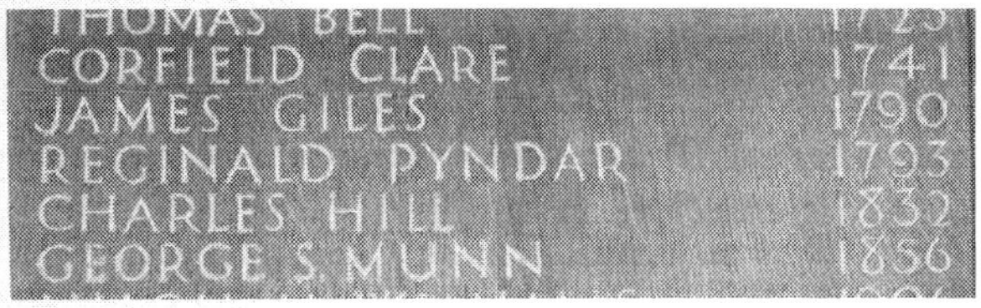

Madresfield Church and a section of the Rectors Board.

The memorial to Charles Hill in Madresfield Churchyard.

Madresfield Court the home of the Lygon/Pyndar family.

One other son-in-law of Rev. Reginald Pyndar, was John Coape Sherbrooke, who was born into the landed gentry at Nottingham in 1764. He joined the army in 1780 as an Ensign in the 1st Foot, and became a Captain in 1783, and Lieutenant Colonel in 1794, during the Napoleonic wars. He served in the Peninsular Campaign with the rank of Lieutenant General, and second in command to Arthur Wellesley, and awarded a KCB in 1809. On the 24th August 1811, Sir John Coape Sherbrooke married Katherina, the eldest daughter of the Rev. Reginald Pyndar, at Areley Kings. In 1811 he was appointed Governor of Nova Scotia, where he arrived with his bride in October 1811. In 1816 he became Governor-in-Chief of British North America. He resigned his commission in 1818, due to ill health and retired to Calverton, where he died in 1830. There are no known children.

Reverend Reginald Pyndar Hill of Bromsberrow (1820-1887)

Reginald Pyndar Hill, the son of Charles Hill of Bromsberrow, was baptised at Bromsberrow and Oldswinford.

Charles Hill was followed by his son the Rev. Reginald Pyndar Hill, who was the Rector from 1856 to 1887, a period of 31 years. He is buried a short distance from his father's grave.

There is also a stained glass window, alongside that of his father's on the south wall, dedicated to the memory of the Rev. Reginald Pyndar Hill by his five children.

William Charles Hill of Bromsberrow (1831-....)

William Charles Hill was the younger son of the Rev. Charles Hill, and brother to the Rev. Reginald Pyndar Hill (above). He is mentioned in the Church records of Madresfield, where he commissioned the decoration of the chancel arch in memory of his grandfather, the Rev. Reginald Pyndar, who was the Rector from 1793-1831, and his father, who was the Rector 1832-1856.

The 1881 census describes him as a military officer, living with his wife, Anna Medoria, aged 46, born at Oxenhall Gloucester, all now living at Powick near Malvern. Further documents, dated 1894 and 1905, describe him as living at The Cottage, Malvern Wells, a Major in the Worcestershire Regiment.

John Hill of Waterford (1749-....)

John was the son of Waldron Hill and his second wife Elizabeth Tyzack, he was baptised 7th September 1749, at Kingswinford. He took over the Ridgegrove Glasshouse in Lye, about 1773 and was the owner of Wordsley Flint Glasshouse in 1776, which was possibly built by him. He married Mary Russell, in 1771 at Oldswinford. They had three children Elizabeth, baptised 21st September 1772, Edward baptised 25th July 1774, and Penelope, baptised 22nd March 1778.

John Hill was hired by the Waterford Glassworks to organise and run the business, which he did, by first recruiting glass craftsmen from Stourbridge. After a dispute he left and went to France.

The Tyzack family were glassmakers, who originated from Lorraine and built the first glasshouse in the district at Lye, called Colemans, which was built by Paul Tyzack around 1612.

Mary Russell, was the daughter of Thomas Russell and niece of Edward Russell, who were also glass manufacturers in Stourbridge, they were also related to the Witton family of Lye, owners of Lye House, (Porridge Hall) by the marriage of Mary Russell, sister of Edward Russell, to Francis Witton.

Edward Russell died in 1778, leaving no issue. His Will *(PRO Prob 11/1046)* left one thousand pounds to John Hill and his wife Mary. His farm, land and other property at Hawbush in Kingswinford, he left to **Elizabeth**, Edward and Penelope, the children of John Hill.

He left his dwelling house, to his niece Elizabeth Witton, and his glasshouse at the Heath, Stourbridge, to his nephews, Francis Witton, Richard Russell Witton and Sargent Witton.

Penelope Hill of Wordsley (1778-....)

Penelope, daughter of John Hill, aged twenty-one, married the Rev. Thomas Hill of Foxcote Farm, at Eastnor Church, 5th April 1799, Curate of Oldswinford Church. She bore him ten children, nine in the twelve years of their marriage and one after his death, on 19th June 1811, their last child Francis, was baptised 1st April 1812, all were born in Lye and all were baptised at Oldswinford, not all survived infancy.

What happened to Penelope, after the death of her husband in 1811, has been the cause of much research, with little or no positive result, with only one possible answer, which at best, is speculation. A Penelope Hill married a Thomas Griffiths, 25th September 1815, at Kidderminster. The daughter of Penelope, Sarah Hill, married Edwin Styles at Hartlebury, 1835, and Martha, another daughter, married Steven Griffiths, 22nd May, 1830 at Cradley.

Francis Hill of Wollaston (1811-....)

Francis was the son of the Rev. Thomas Hill of Foxcote and Penelope. Born in Lye after his father's death, and baptised 1812 at Oldswinford. He was probably brought up by his uncle Francis at Foxcote Farm and was a beneficiary of his will. He was found living in the High Street, Wollaston, in 1881 aged 70, a Colliery Clerk, with his wife Susannah aged 71, and an unmarried son, called **Thomas Waldron Hill,** aged 47, born at Belbroughton, who was an Auctioneer's Clerk, and a granddaughter named **Rhoda**, aged 9, born Stourbridge, and also a niece, Mary Waldron, aged 15, a scholar, born at Upper Sapey, Worcester.

Rhoda Frances Ellen Hill was baptised 31st December 1871, at Oldswinford, she was the daughter of **Francis** and Elizabeth Hill, and the granddaughter of Francis Hill above.

Sarah Hopkins Hill (1810-....)

Sarah was the daughter of the Rev. Thomas Hill of Foxcote, she was one year old, when her father died. She was born at Lye and baptised Sarah on the 22nd February 1810, at Oldswinford, but when she married Edwin Styles, 10th February 1835, at Hartlebury, she was Sarah Hopkins Hill, named after Sarah Hopkins of Rugeley.

Reverend Edward Hill of Hindley (1774-1853)

Edward was at Queen's College, Oxford in 1797, he was mentioned in the will of Edward Russell in 1778, uncle of his mother, he was probably there at the same time as the Rev. Thomas Hill, (above), who was two years his senior, and also at Queen's College, Oxford in 1791. The Rev. Edward Hill, is also mentioned in the will of Sarah Hopkins, who describes him as her cousin and being of Hindley, Lancaster in 1844.

The Rev. Edward Hill, and his sisters Elizabeth and Penelope, were left Hawbush Farm by the will of Edward Russell, who was their great uncle. Elizabeth died, her share passing to her brother, as heir at law. In May 1797, Hawbush Farm was sold to Thomas Wheeley of Kingswinford, Glassmaker, for Two Thousand Pounds, which was divided between them, with two thirds to Edward and one third to Penelope. Witnesses to the deed were Waldron Hill and Thomas Hill.

Edward was the Vicar of All Saints Parish Church, Hindley,[1] from 1830 to 1853, where he died in 1853 aged 79.

All Saints Parish Church, Hindley.

The Church, built in 1641 was originally a Presbyterian Chapel, and is still referred to as the Chapel, it served both Presbyterian and Anglican communities until 1662, when

[1] Map Ref SO 622 043

it became an Anglican Church. It was consecrated in 1698, on All Saints Day as the Parish Church of All Saints, Hindley, and rebuilt in brick in 1766/7.

Reverend Henry William Hill of Rock (1782-1840)

The Rev. Henry William Hill, son of Thomas Hill of Dennis and his wife Anne Melsup, was the Rector of St. Peter's and St. Paul's Church[1], for twenty-eight years, which is the Parish Church of Rock in Worcestershire. He married Susanna Still Brettell in 1809, at Kingswinford, daughter of Thomas Brettell, a Stourbridge solicitor, they had eight known children.

Rev Henry William married Susanna Brettell

Anne	Emma	Henry Thomas	James Charles	Melsup	Peter	Susan	Marrianne
1811	1813	1814	1815	1818			1827

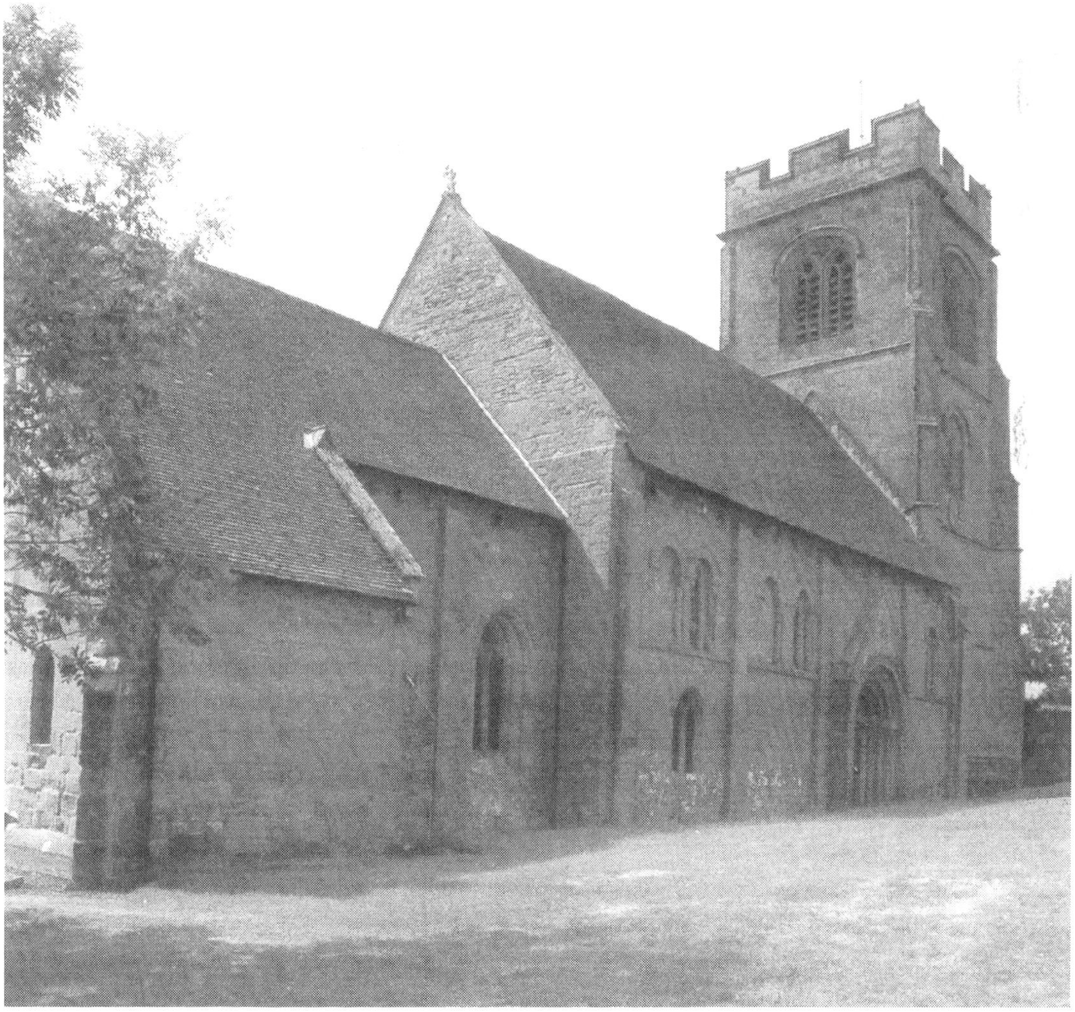

Saint Peter's and Saint Paul's Church at Rock.

[1] Map Ref SO 732 712

He died 3rd April 1840, aged 58. A tablet, erected by his widow and children, in his memory, can be found on the north wall in the chancel, and also a stained glass window in memory of him and his wife Susanna Still, who died 7th January 1860.

THIS TABLET
IS PLACED HERE BY THE
SORROWING WIDOW AND CHILDREN OF THE
REVEREND HENRY WILLIAM HILL
FOR XXVIII YEARS
RECTOR OF THIS PARISH
NEAR TO THIS SPOT THEY HAVE LAID FOR
IMMORTALITY ALL THAT WAS MORTAL.
HE DIED APRIL THE IIIRD MDCCCXL
AGED LVIII

HIS END WAS PEACE

BLESSED ARE THE MERCIFUL FOR THEY
SHALL OBTAIN MERCY MATT V. VER V11

The Church is of Norman origin, built around 1160, other parts being built in the late 13th Century, the walls are quite sparse and bare, with little in the way of memorial tablets. The village stocks and whipping post were said to be sited near by, but appear to have fallen out of use and have disappeared!

The grave of Henry William is close to the church, but could not be found.

It is here at Rock that his sons Henry Thomas, and Melsup were born. Henry Thomas and Melsup, went into church service and were at differing times the Incumbents at Christ Church, Lye.

The will *(PRO Prob 11/1945)* of the Rev. Henry William Hill, was made the 13th March 1840, and was proved 5th May 1841, it was short and to the point, leaving every thing to his wife, naming her and his son, the Rev. Henry Thomas as Executrix and Executor.

The stained glass window dedicated to Henry William Hill and his wife Susanna Still.

Reverend Henry Thomas Hill of Felton (1814-1882)

The Rev. Henry Thomas Hill became the first Incumbent of Christ Church, Lye in 1839, after the dismissal of John Hodgson, which he held until 1843. He was then, followed by his brother, Melsup, who held the post for a similar period. From 1843 to 1851, he was Curate at the Church of St. John the Baptist at Wolverley.

Henry Thomas married Ursula Frances Bund, 6th October 1841, at St. Mary's Church, Great Malvern. A Ursula Frances Bund, was baptised in 1818 at Wick Church near Worcester, daughter of Thomas Henry Bund and Anne Wilmot.

Their children were, Walter Wilmot, born about 1844, and given his grandmother's maiden name, **Gerard**, who died 13th April 1855, and **Henry W B**, who died 27th February 1856; who are remembered, by two pairs of identical stained glass windows on the south wall of Felton Church, and Herbert Francis who died in 1911, and is remember by a brass plate, there was also an **Arthur Felton**.

In 1851 Henry Thomas became the Rector of the Church of St. Michael the Archangel in the Parish of Felton[1], where he served for thirty years, and also Vicar of the neighbouring Parish of Preston Wynne, at the Holy Trinity Church, in 1858, he was also Dean of North Froome.

Felton is between Bromyard and Hereford, and the Church can be found down a narrow lane that passes through a farmyard to reveal the Church behind.

The Church of Saint Michael the Archangel in the Parish of Felton.

[1] Map Ref SO 579 485.

The church was rebuilt in 1853-4 at a cost of £1280, including five bells. The earliest register is 1650.
The present pulpit, made of marble, was given to the Church in memory of Henry Thomas Hill, by friends and neighbours. The rectory is on adjoining land.

Ursula died 17th February 1877, and Henry Thomas died 11th January 1882, they are buried in the churchyard.

The 1881 census, shows Henry Thomas Hill remarried Harriet S, aged 52, who was born in East Kingsmouth, Devon and described as the Rectors wife.

The marble pulpit, in memory of the Rev. Henry Thomas Hill.

Preston Wynne is a small village, off the beaten track, deep in the Herefordshire countryside, it can only be found by negotiating a series of narrow lanes. The village itself, possibly best described as 'quaint', has no post office, public house, shop or any other amenity. It has stables, three farms, a hop farm and a number of timber barns in a dilapidated condition. It is a place that time has forgotten, a complete time warp, whose only contact with the outside world is by car, telephone or television. The village contains many half-timbered buildings.

Derelict barn at Preston Wynne.

The Holy Trinity Church at Preston Wynne.

The Holy Trinity Church at Preston Wynne[1], has its own Churchyard, was originally built in 1727, and rebuilt in 1858; it has a tower with one bell. It can be found amongst the fields, and can only be reached by a stile and a walk across the fields, of 200 to 300 yards, through either a flock of sheep or a herd of cows. The Church is still in use; its interior is small, plain and simple. There is no road or path to it, people attending weddings or funerals either have to walk, or use other vehicles suitable to the terrain. The surrounding fields are laid out with wires and poles for the production of hops.

The hop farm or yard, near the village, still has the living quarters of the hop-pickers, who occupied them many years ago.

The Rev. Henry Thomas Hill, M.A. of Corpus Christi College, Cambridge, Rector of Felton and Vicar of Preston Wynne, was also a Prebendary[2] of Nunnington in Herefordshire Cathedral, and was one of the main land owners in the district.

In 1870 Henry Thomas built a school[3] at Preston Wynne, at a cost of £320, on land he owned, to accommodate 36 children of both parishes, which existed, as a school, up to 1972, it is now a privately owned house. There is approximately one mile between the two churches.

---

[1] Map Ref SO 558 466
[2] Honorary canon.
[3] Map Ref SO 564 470

The old school built in 1870, by The Rev. Henry Thomas Hill at a cost of £320, and the school motto, over the window on the extreme left, enlarged and shown below. Note the upside down **W**!

The population of Felton was 149 in 1867, and 127 in 1871, and Preston Wynne had a population of 182 in 1861, and 172 in 1871, it is doubtful if there is much change in the population today!

Reverend Walter Wilmot Hill (about 1844-1888)

The Rev. Walter Wilmot Hill, was born about 1844 at Wolverley, he was the son of Henry Thomas Hill. Walter Wilmot was the Vicar of St. James the Great Church at Ocle Pychard[1], Herefordshire, for twelve years. He died in 1888 and is buried in the churchyard; a stained glass window is dedicated to him on the south wall.
The Church, is close to the Churches of Felton and Preston Wynne, previously mentioned, and served by the Rev. Henry Thomas Hill, who built the Rectory here at

The Church of Saint James the Great, Ocle Pychard.

Ocle Pychard. The original Church was probably built in the late 12 century and has undergone many changes. At one time it had a thatched roof and the present steeple is covered with copper. The Tower has three bells. The name of the village comes from two family surnames of Oakley and Pychard. Part of the Rectors board is shown here on the right, it shows the Rev. Hopkins Hill, (mentioned on page 40) who was the Vicar here for 24 years and his distant cousin Walter Wilmot Hill.

---

[1] Map Ref SO 596 463

Thomas Hill (3) of Rudall, near Ross, was the Patron of Felton and Ocle Pychard during the term of office of Hopkins Hill. The population, during the period of office by both of the Hills, was about 300. The Rev. Henry Thomas Hill was its patron during the term of office of his son, Walter Wilmot Hill.

The Rev. Henry Thomas Hill was the first incumbent at Lye Church, 1839 to 1843, and then Curate at Wolverley, 1843 to 1851 and finally, Rector of Felton, from 1851 until 1882, and Vicar at the nearby Parish Church of Preston Wynne.
This picture of him shown here, is from a painting, which hangs in the Church at Ocle Pychard.

Herbert Francis Hill of Scalby (1850-1911)

Herbert Francis was the son of Henry Thomas and Ursula Hill, he was born at Wolverley. A brass plaque in Felton Church is dedicated to Herbert Francis Hill, Lieutenant Colonel of the 1st Essex Regiment (44th) who died at Scalby, Yorkshire 9th April 1911, aged 61.
There is a further plaque in memory of his wife Mary, daughter of John Leader of Keale Co. Cork, born February 18th 1850 – Died March 10th 1931. Also of **Dorothy Mary Joyce** their beloved younger daughter who died October 6th 1900 aged 11.

The old memorial hall just outside the main village of Preston Wynne, serves as a community centre for both villages.

Captain Gerard Leader Hill (1882-1917)

Gerard Leader Hill, was the son of Lieutenant Colonel Herbert Francis Hill and grandson of the Rev. Henry Thomas Hill. A brass plaque in Felton Church is dedicated to him, the wording is shown below.

TO THE GLORY OF GOD
IN PROUD MEMORY OF
CAPTAIN GERARD LEADER HILL
2/5TH LINCOLNSHIRE REGIMENT
ONLY SON OF THE LATE
LIEUT. COLONEL HERBERT FRANCIS HILL
AND MARY HIS WIFE
KILLED IN ACTION AT THE 3RD BATTLE OF YPRES
SEPTEMBER 26TH 1917, AGED 35 YEARS
DULCE ET DECORUM EST PRO PATRIA MORI[1]

The 3rd Battle of Ypres was probably better known as Passchendaele. It began on the 31st July 1817 with a barrage, which lasted for 10 days, firing four and a half million shells, which completely destroyed the drainage system of the area of combat, the subsequent heavy rain that followed turned the battle field into a sea of mud.

Military intelligence was well aware, beforehand, of the consequences of such a barrage, and of the heavy rain forecasted for the region, they also knew that the Germans had knowledge of the forthcoming offensive and were waiting in readiness, but in spite of knowing the odds were stacked against him, Haig was determined to push on with the offensive.

At first the advance was quite promising, but soon became bogged down by the mud and the defence system used by the Germans. The use of mustard gas and the strafing of the troops by the German Air Force, further hampered the advance, causing further casualties. It became slaughter of the highest magnitude, even by military standards.

Finally, British troops captured Passchendaele Ridge and Passchendaele village, on the 6th November, extending the salient by five miles, at a cost of 300,000 British, 8,500 French and 260,000 German lives.

---

[1] From the famous poem by Wilfred Owen "Dulce et decorum est".
The last line of which, reads, 'The old lie: Dulce et decorum est pro patria mori' its translation is **'It is sweet and meet to die for one's country. Sweet! and decorous!'** This line was amended by Wilfred Owen and replaced with 'Of gas shells dropping softly that dropped behind....' and was considered to be unfinished.

Reverend Melsup Hill of Shelsey Beuchamp (1818-1887)

The Rev. Melsup Hill son of the Rev. Henry William Hill of Rock, Incumbent at Christ Church, Lye, from 1843 to 1846, where he was not as popular as his brother, who had previously held the post, it was said he had been stoned out of Lye, which was sad, but tends to confirm the description given of Lye folk in these times by various observers.

All Saints Church at Shelsley Beauchamp.

His son, also called Melsup, was found on the 1881 census living at Leeds, where he was described as a schoolmaster MA, who must have had a cultured accent, as the Enumerator entered him on the census as being born in 'Laye' near Stourbridge. If the accent of the Rev. Melsup was similar that of his son, one can understand why the folk's of Lye disliked him! He was more popular in the Parish of Shelsey Beauchamp, where he was Rector for thirty years, from 1857 to 1887. He was followed by the Rev. William Griffiths, previously the Vicar of the Parish Church of All Saints, Sedgley from 1876 to 1888.

All Saints Church, at Shelsley Beauchamp[1] is an old church, its earliest Rector recorded as 1320.

The Rev. Melsup Hill appears to have married three times, all his children were baptised by Melsup and Rose, who Rose was and when they were married is not known. Their first child was Melsup, who must have been born at Lye in 1845-6. After his ejection from Lye, the Rev. Melsup appears to have moved to Kidderminster, where some of his children were baptised, they were **Mary Katharine** 1846, **Thomas** 1849 and **Susan Rose** 1852, all were baptised at St. John the Baptist Church, Kidderminster. He then moved to Shelsley Beauchamp, where **Blanche** was

[1] Map Ref SO 731 628

baptised in 1859. He married Susan Elizabeth Corrie 27th April 1865, at St. James Church, Paddington, London. The 1881 census for Shelsley Beauchamp shows his wife as Sarah Elizabeth Hill, aged sixty-nine, born at Handsworth, Stafford, and Melsup born Rock, aged sixty-three.

The brass plaque shown here is dedicated to the memory of the Rev. Melsup Hill, it can be found in the lych gate to the Church.

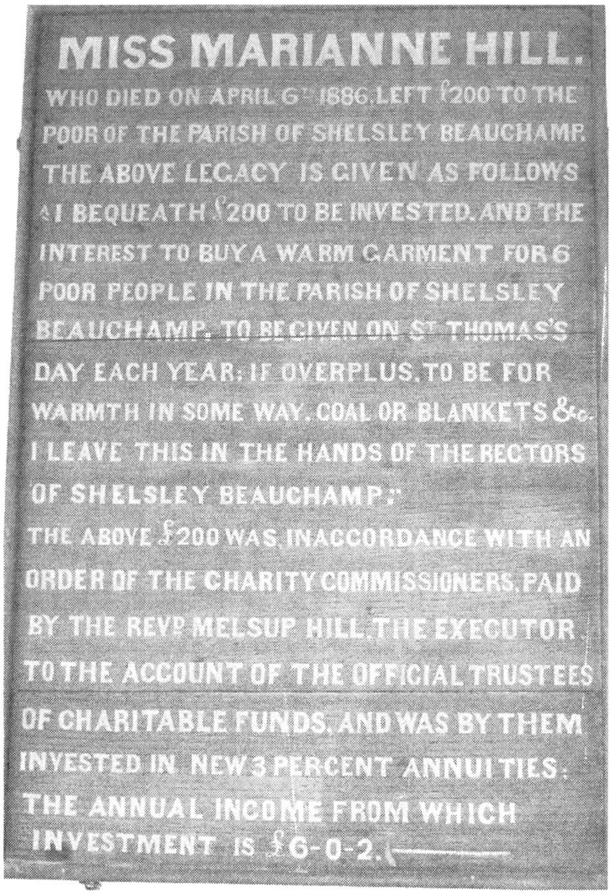

Marianne Hill of Rock and Shelsey Beauchamp (1827-1886)

Marianne Hill was the daughter of the Rev. Henry William Hill, Rector of Rock, and the sister of Melsup. There is a Beneficiary board in Shelsey Beauchamp Church, dedicated to her, for leaving £200 in her will, to help the poor of the village, where she appears to have been living when she died.

The parish pump at Shelsey Beauchamp, with All Saints Church in the background.

James Charles Hill (1815-....)

James Charles Hill was the second eldest son of the Rev. Henry William, baptised at Rock, 9th Augsust 1815, he was an iron master. He married Elizabeth Crawshay, in 1855 at Awre with Blakenley, Gloucestershire, daughter of Henry Crawshay, an iron master at Abergavenny. He bought the Govilon Forge in 1858, and made his fortune. He retired in 1870 to his house called 'The Brooks' and became High Sheriff of Monmouthshire in 1872.

Reverend Thomas Hill of Foxcote (1772-1811)

Oldswinford Church about 1832, where the Rev. Thomas Hill was Curate until 1811. Note the stocks to the left of the gate. (Picture from the Stourbridge Library Collection).

Whilst Lye did not have a church until 1813, it did have a Curate who was the Rev. Thomas Hill born at Foxcote, son of Francis Hill senior, brother to Mary Penn and Francis junior, he was the Curate at St. Mary's Church[1] Oldswinford for sixteen years. He married Penelope Hill, at Eastnor[2] 5th April 1799. All of his children were born in Lye and baptised at Oldswinford Church. Thomas died suddenly on the 19th June 1811, aged 39, leaving his wife with a number of children under the age of ten and a further child on the way. It is believed that Francis, his brother, assisted with the upbringing of a number of the children at Foxcote Farm[3].

Marianne (Hill) Brook of Foxcote (1804-....)

Marianne Hill was the daughter of the Rev. Thomas Hill and his wife Penelope, she was probably living at Foxcote with her uncle Francis, where she met William Brook the nephew of Hannah, wife of Francis Hill. They were later married at Great Malvern, 17th June 1835. The timing of their marriage may have been influenced by the death of Francis Hill, who died in 1835. His will was made 28th March 1835, and proved 29th October 1835, of which Marianne and William were both beneficiaries.

---

[1] Map Ref SO 908 832
[2] Map Ref SO 731 372
[3] Map Ref SO 932 836

The 1841 census show Marianne and William Brook and their two children, **Nancy,** aged three and **Eliza,** aged one, living at Foxcote Farm, with their aunt Hannah. Marianne and William Brook, and their two children, were also shown living at Oldnall Farm. William was probably the farm manager for Francis Hill. Hannah Hill died late 1841. Some time after the death of Francis Hill, Thomas Pargeter took over the farm, followed by his daughter Caroline Elizabeth. William Brook appears to have been farm manager for the Pargeters and was rewarded in their wills.

Saint Mary's Church, Oldswinford as it is today.

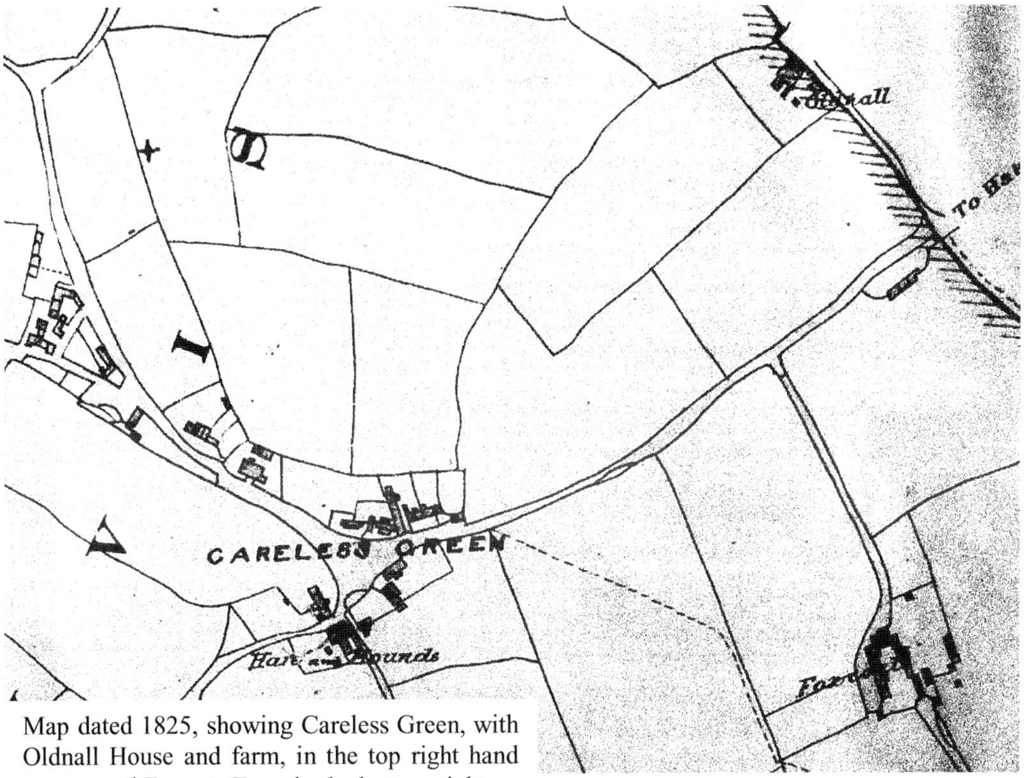

Map dated 1825, showing Careless Green, with Oldnall House and farm, in the top right hand corner, and Foxcote Farm in the bottom right.

Mary Penn (Hill) Bagley of Foxcote or Oldnall (1763-....)

Mary Penn Hill was the sister of Francis Hill and the Rev. Thomas Hill; she married Dudley Bagley (jun) of Bagley's Mill[1] in 1791. The mill was partly a blade mill, where probably her brother Francis ground some of his scythes. They had nine children between 1792 and 1805, all were baptised at Oldswinford, most were mentioned in the will of her brother Francis.

The Bagley family occupied the mill from 1785, taking over from the Richards family, until 1822, working it as a blade mill, possibly making scythes, and a corn mill. The mill became known as Bagley's Mill, but was often called Lye mill, although the mill was actually in Amblecote.

Dudley Bagley senior, died 14th May 1815, aged 88 and was buried at Sedgley, where he had been living for some time at Ettingshall Park, the home of his daughter Ann.

The Bagleys, whilst being well documented and associated with Lye, was a Sedgley family. Both Dudley (sen) born 1727, and Dudley (jun) born 1762, were born at Sedgley, where the Bagleys had lived for generations and to where a number of the family returned after their lease with the mill expired. The Bagley name first appeared in the Sedgley records in 1542.

The Bagley family owned the land at Sedgley, where the Work House once stood, and the road near by, called Dibdale Lane, was known as Bagley's Lane.

Dudley Bagley (sen), was the son of Jevon Ashenhurst Bagley and Elizabeth Marsh, he married Ann Jones 28th May 1757, at St. Bartholomew's Church, Wednesbury. They had three children, Dudley, John Marsh and Ann. Dudley married Mary Penn Hill, John Marsh died aged 19 and Ann married Samuel Feraday of Sedgley.

Samuel Feraday was the son of Samuel Feraday of Upper Gornal. Samuel Feraday (sen) was described on deeds dated 1760 and 1790, as a stone cutter and stone mason. He was in fact a quarry master, working the stone quarries of Upper Gornal, obtaining stone to line the blast furnaces in the surrounding district. Samuel Feraday (jun), married Ann Bagley, the only daughter of Dudley Bagley of Bagley's Mill, Lye, on the 17th October 1782, at Aston Juxta, Birmingham, he was described as a farmer of Park Farm, Sedgley.

Samuel Feraday of Upper Gornal, stone cutter, became the owner of the Rewardine Wind Mill on 23rd February 1760. An Indenture, dated 23rd March 1790, transferred the mill, then in the occupation of William Turton, to his son Samuel Feraday (jun) of Park Farm, farmer, who became the husband of Ann Bagley. Samuel Feraday (jun) disposed of the mill, on the 24th December 1795, to Benjamin Lloyde and Thomas Turner the Parish Miller.

Samuel (jun), became one of the richest iron and coal masters of his time, owning blast furnaces and ironworks at Priestfield and Bradley etc., living at Ettingshall Park,

---

[1] Map Ref SO 914 847

where, after the victory at Waterloo, he gave an enormous party for 1500 of his work force, this figure swelled to 3000 with additional invitations to the poor of the district.

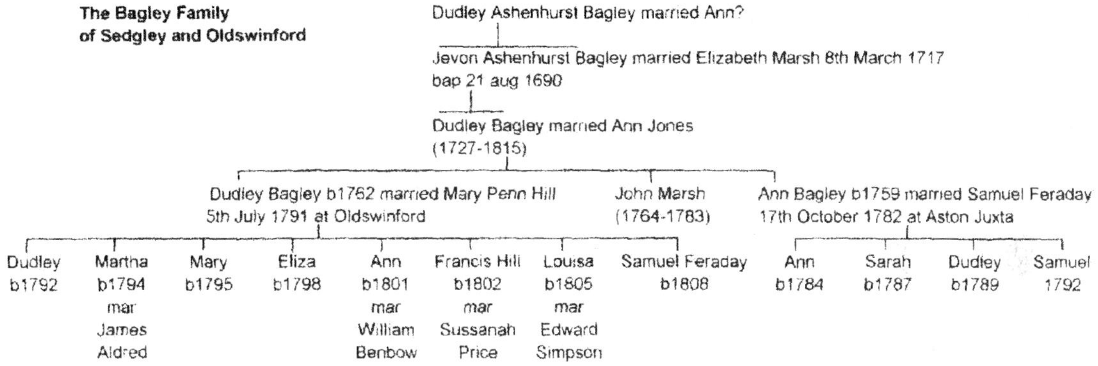

Samuel and Ann had three children, Ann 1784, Sarah 1787 and Dudley 1789, another son, Samuel died in infancy in 1792. Their son Dudley became quite famous.
Dudley Feraday was privately educated and went to Magdalene College, Oxford in 1811, and obtained an honorary degree of M.A. in 1814.
Following the peace there was a depression in the iron and coal industry, Samuel Feraday became bankrupt. Because of the state of the industry and his father's bankruptcy, Dudley was forced to seek employment elsewhere. He sought the help of Lord Hatherton, who obtained a situation for him in Sierra Leone, but after a few years he came home sick and exhausted. After recovery, he again sought help from Lord Hatherton, who obtained for him, the office of High Sheriff of Van Diemen's Land (Tasmania), where he obtained considerable property. After a number of years he returned home to Ettingshall Park, where he remained until his death in 1849.

Van Dieman's land, at this time, was an Australian colony, where thousands of British subjects were being transported for minor crimes, the main purpose being to populate the Australian Colonies, and provide a cheap labour force for building roads and bridges etc.

"The Fatal Shore", the book by Robert Hughes on convictry, describes in vivid detail the suffering of the convicts sent to Van Dieman's Land[1], he also describes Dudley Feraday, on page 393 as follows: "Arthur[2] made no bones about the scope of his patronage or his bias toward military men, given the quality of some of the civil officials the Crown sent, one can hardly blame him. Dudley Feraday (1789-1849) a bankrupt coal magnate's son whom an English Lord's patronage had made sheriff of Van Dieman's Land in 1824 turned out to be a relentless usurer, lending money at 35 percent interest. Arthur soon got rid of him and of his incompliant attorney-general, Arthur Gellibrand, and of anyone else who seemed either disobliging or short on moral fibre".

Dudley Feraday, unmarried, died in 1849, leaving £20,000 to Magdalene College for the founding of four fellowships.

---

[1] The author's great, great, grandfather was sent to Van Dieman's Land as a convict in 1845 on board the sailing ship Mayda.
[2] Sir George Arthur, Governor of Van Diemans Land.

The will *(PRO Prob 11/1571)* of Dudley Bagley left to his daughter Ann Feraday, and her husband Samuel Feraday, who he is presumed to have been living with prior to his death, since he describes himself as living at Ettingshall Park. There is no mention of his son Dudley, or his daughter-in-law Mary Penn, or his grandchildren by them; one must assume he had made provision for them before his death?

A marble tablet on the north wall of All Saints Church, Sedgley[1] reads, "In memory of DUDLEY BAGLEY who died 14th of May 1815. Aged 88 years. Also of ANN BAGLEY who died 2nd July 1800. Aged 73 years. Likewise of JOHN MARSH, son of Dudley and Ann Bagley; who died May 6th 1783. Aged 19 years. This Tablet was Erected by his only daughter Anne Feraday of Ettingshall Park, in the year of our Lord 1823.
Further proof, should it be required, of the Bagley family links with Sedgley, can be found in the Family tree of Mary Penn (Hill) Bagley, who baptised her son Samuel Feraday, and her sister-in-law Ann Feraday (Bagley) named her son Dudley.

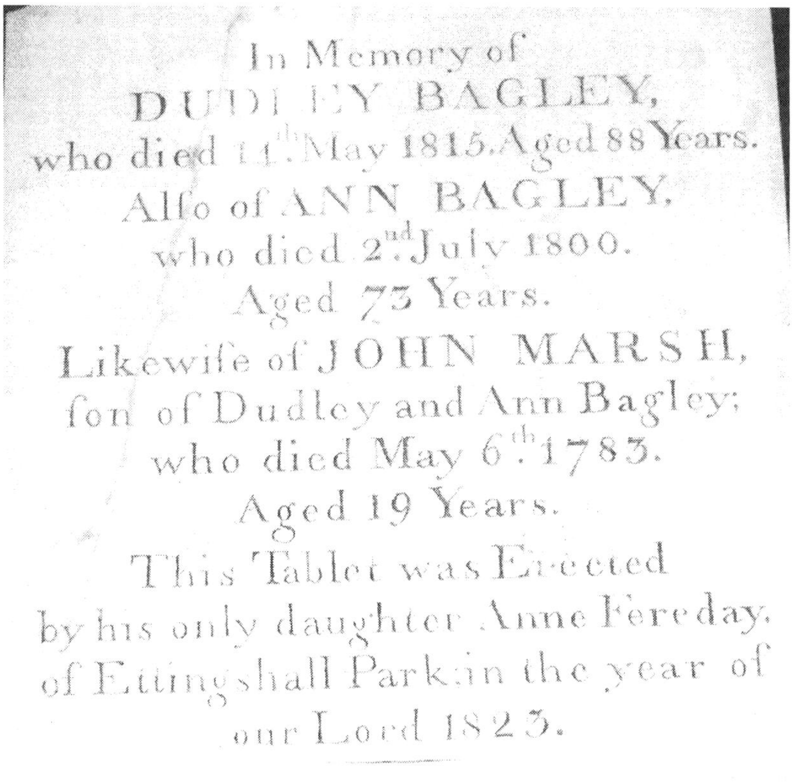

This marble tablet can be found at on the north wall of All Saints Church, Sedgley.

The following are extracts taken from a book dated 1898, called "Sedgley Resources" by F. W. Hackwood, it refers to the Bagley and Hill families.

(b) 10 and 11 June, 1791. Indentures of Lease and Re-lease made between Dudley Bagley and Ann, his wife, Dudley Bagley, the younger, eldest son and heir-apparent of the said Dudley Bagley, the elder, by Ann, his wife, of the first part; Mary Penn Hill, spinster, of the second part: Francis Hill, of Dennis, in the hamlet of Amblecot, in the County of Stafford, Esq, and Francis Hill, of Foxcote, Oldswinford, Gent, and Thomas Hill, of Queen's College, Oxford, Gent., of the 3rd part; and Benjamin Bagley, farmer, of the 4th part, being a settlement of hereditaments in contemplation of a marriage which was then intended to be solemnized between Dudley Bagley, the son and Mary Penn Hill.

(c) 22 and 23 December, 1813. – Dudley Bagley (the son) deposed of his life estate in the hereditaments.

---

[1] Map Ref 917 936

Francis Hill Bagley, of Dibdale, Sedgley, farmer was the eldest son of Dudley Bagley, by Mary Penn, his wife, and he and six younger children by the same marriage were alive on the 2nd January, 1835, when, by a mortgage deed made between Francis Hill, of Foxcote, Gent, of the first part, the said Francis Hill Bagley of the 2nd part, and Francis Walker, of Stourbridge, of the 3rd part, the hereditaments were mortgaged by F. H. Bagley to Francis Walker for £1,500. In September 1840, they were further charged with £500 to Mr. Walker.

On January 6th, 1849, the properties were sold to Dudley Fereday of Ettingshall Park, Sedgley, Esq., by the mortgages of F. H. Bagley.

Mr. Blocksidge, in his Notes on St. Edmund's Registers, Dudley, says the name of Bagley appears 21 times from 1540 to 1611, the first entry being July 1542; page 3.

In attempting to determine the meaning of the above passages, the following notes might be of some assistance.
Mary Penn Hill married Dudley Bagley 5th July 1791.
Section *(b)* made 10th and 11th of June 1791, is part of the marriage settlement made just prior to the marriage.
Francis Hill of Dennis, is the father of Mary Penn. He would now be about 61 years of age, and had previously been living at Foxcote, but now lives at Dennis, the house of his cousin Thomas Hill, who might be away at Blaenavon.
Thomas Hill of Queens College, Oxford, is Mary's 19-year old brother, who became the Rev. Thomas Hill, Curate at Oldswinford Church and died aged 39.

Section *(c)* made in 1813, between Francis Hill Bagley and his uncle Francis Hill, when the property *(hereditaments)* were mortgaged to Francis Walker to raise £1500.

The will of Francis Hill, who died 1835, leaving property in Sedgley, to his nephew Francis Hill Bagley, who still appears to be having financial difficulties, forcing him to mortgage it, which on the 6th of January 1849, is bought by his cousin Dudley Fereday of Ettingshall Park.

Francis Hill (2) of Foxcote (1760-1835)

Francis Hill, Farmer and Scythesmith, son of Francis Hill senior, lived at Foxcote Farm, he was born at Foxcote Farm or Oldnall Farm. He married Hannah Brook, spinster, at Kinver in 1800, she was born at Kinver in 1761. Both were about 40 years of age at the time of their marriage, there are no known children from their marriage.

Francis, like his father before him, was a scythesmith, carrying on his business at the Stamber Mill[1], which was a hammer forge, and Shepherds Brook Mill, which was a blade mill, grinding the scythe blades, which they leased from the Hickmans. It is also thought that there was a business relationship between Francis and Dudley Bagley of Bagley's Mill, which blossomed into a marriage between Mary Penn Hill, Francis's sister, and Dudley Bagley junior.

[1] Map Ref SO 914 845

The will *(PRO Prob 11/1853)* of Francis, who died in 1835, left to his wife, Hannah, his sister, Mary Penn Bagley, and her children (nieces and nephews), the children of his brother the Rev. Thomas Hill (deceased), Curate of Oldswinford Church, and William Brook the nephew of his wife. William Brook married Marianne, daughter of the Rev. Thomas Hill.

His will tells us more about his involvement in other businesses.
He left his mill at Bedcoat[1] (Stourbridge), on the Stour, to his niece **Martha Bagley**, wife of James Aldred miller, and his two leasehold furnaces, presumably iron furnaces, at Grave Yard, Dibdale and two pieces of land, he left to his nephews **Francis Hill Bagley**, a farmer at Dibdale (Sedgley), and **Samuel Feraday Bagley**, a surgeon at Dibdale. Two thousand pounds in trust to his four nieces, **Mary Bagley, Eliza Bagley, Ann Bagley** and **Louisa Bagley**, sisters of Martha. His numerous buildings and appurtenances in Careless Green, he left to his niece Marianne and his wife's nephew William Brook, and £40 per year to his sister Mary Penn Bagley. His farm and lands, were to be sold and put into trust by the trustees, who were Thomas Bates and William Robins, Bankers of Stourbridge. Other beneficiaries were **Francis Hill, Martha Hill, Elizabeth Hill** and **Sarah Hopkins Hill**, who were the son and daughters of the Rev. Thomas Hill.

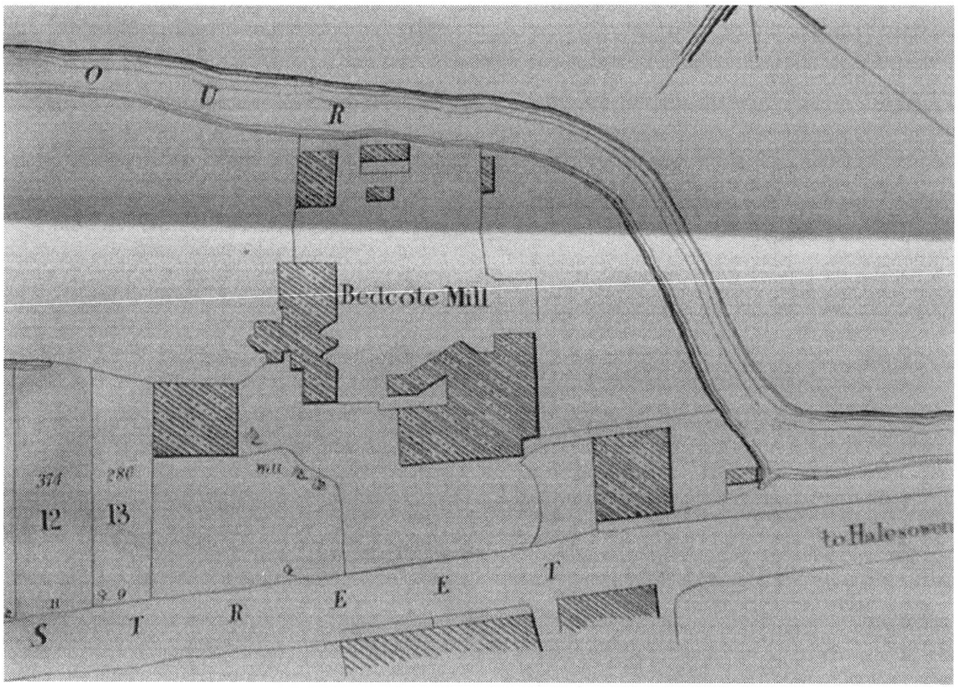

Bedcote Mill 1851.

In 1851 Bedcote Mill was a steam driven flourmill, equipped with a 15-horse power steam engine, turning four pairs of stones, complete with cart and hackney stables, and land having an area of three acres. It was in the occupation of Edwin Blundell, and was auctioned at the Talbot Inn, Stourbridge, on the 9th December 1851.

There were two Bedcote Mills, upper and lower, only a short distance apart, the one described above was the lower Bedcote Mill, the upper Bedcote Mill was closer to the viaduct and known as a corn mill.

[1] Map Ref SO 905 846

The land mentioned above, was bought by Francis Hill for £540 from the Hickman family[1], in part exchange for land, owned by Francis, close to the Castle at Oldswinford, which was the home of the Hickmans.

He also left "£10 in trust to be invested, and the interest there from, to be used for the Lye school founded by my Family and applied for charitable purposes of the school".

Two of the Executors to the will of Francis Hill, were the Rev. William Blow Collis and Thomas Pargeter, and two of the witnesses were, Joseph Hancox Pargeter and William Perrins, of Careless Green.

Thomas Pargeter (1766-1849), married his cousin Caroline Pargeter, they occupied/owned Foxcote Farm, sometime after the death of Francis Hill and the death of his wife Hannah in 1842.

Joseph Hancox Pargeter (1812-1836), lived at Careless Green House, he died shortly after signing the will of Francis Hill, aged twenty-four.

William Perrins owned 'The Hare and Hounds', and was the brother of Thomas Perrins, owner of the chain works in Careless Green.

Melsup Hill of 'Laye' (1845-....)

Melsup Hill born in 'Laye', near Stourbridge, was a School Teacher, aged 35, unmarried, with an M.A., and was found on the 1881 census, living in a Boarding House in Leeds. Whilst his accent must have been very refined, he was obviously born in Lye 1845-6 and the son of the Rev. Melsup Hill.

There is still many more questions remaining, one in particular, is, where were the Hill family of Oldnall making their scythes? We know John Hill of Foxcote (about 1724-1758), was a third generation scythesmith of the Hill family, who in his will said "I desire my brother Francis Hill to have the benefit of the trade of scythesmith which I have carried on", and we also know that an Indenture made 21st February 1814, between Martha Hickman, then owner of the Stamber Mill, and Joseph Fellows[2], mentions the mill as "All that Forge and Mill heretobefore a Blade Mill but since converted to a Hammer Forge called Stomber Mill Forge with all erection Shops Buildings and appurtenances to the same belonging also all that Blade Mill situate and being near to the said Forge and also the two pools or ponds belonging to the said Forge and Blade Mill with the two water wheels all of which have previously been in the tenure or occupation of Francis Hill".

It would seem likely that the Hills used the Stamber Mill Forge to make their scythes and the Shepherds Brook Mill to grind them, but their occupation of these two mills ceased before Joseph Fellows, an oatmeal maker, took over the lease, resulting in them moving to Bagley's Mill, as mentioned above, where they continued until the death of Francis Hill.

---

[1] See pages 48 and 140 of "The Hickmans of Oldswinford" by M.V.Herbert.
[2] See "A Brief History of Lye and Wollescote" by Don Cochrane.

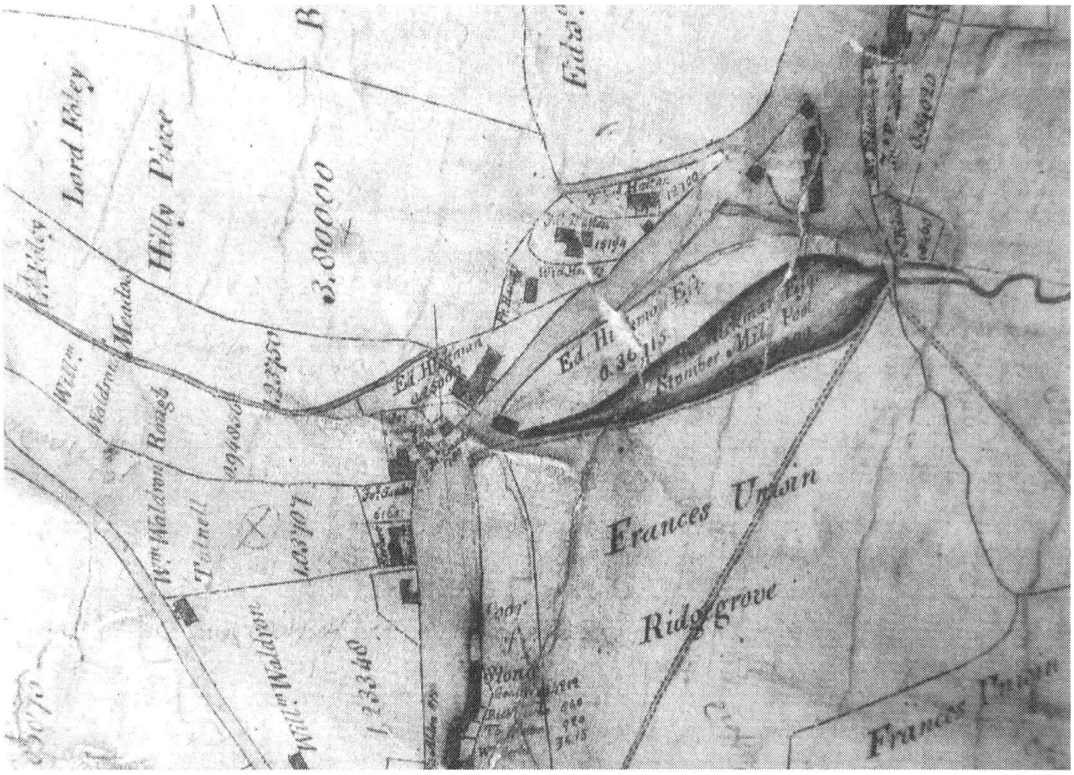

The map above, drawn by Harry Court in 1782, shows the main road from Lye to Stourbridge, and the Stamber Mill, which is the 'L' shaped building, centre left, with the 'tail race' coming from behind. The mill pool is on the opposite side of the road, shown as 'Stumber Mill Pool', owned by Edward Hickman. Note the three pieces of land in the bottom left hand corner owned by William Waldron.

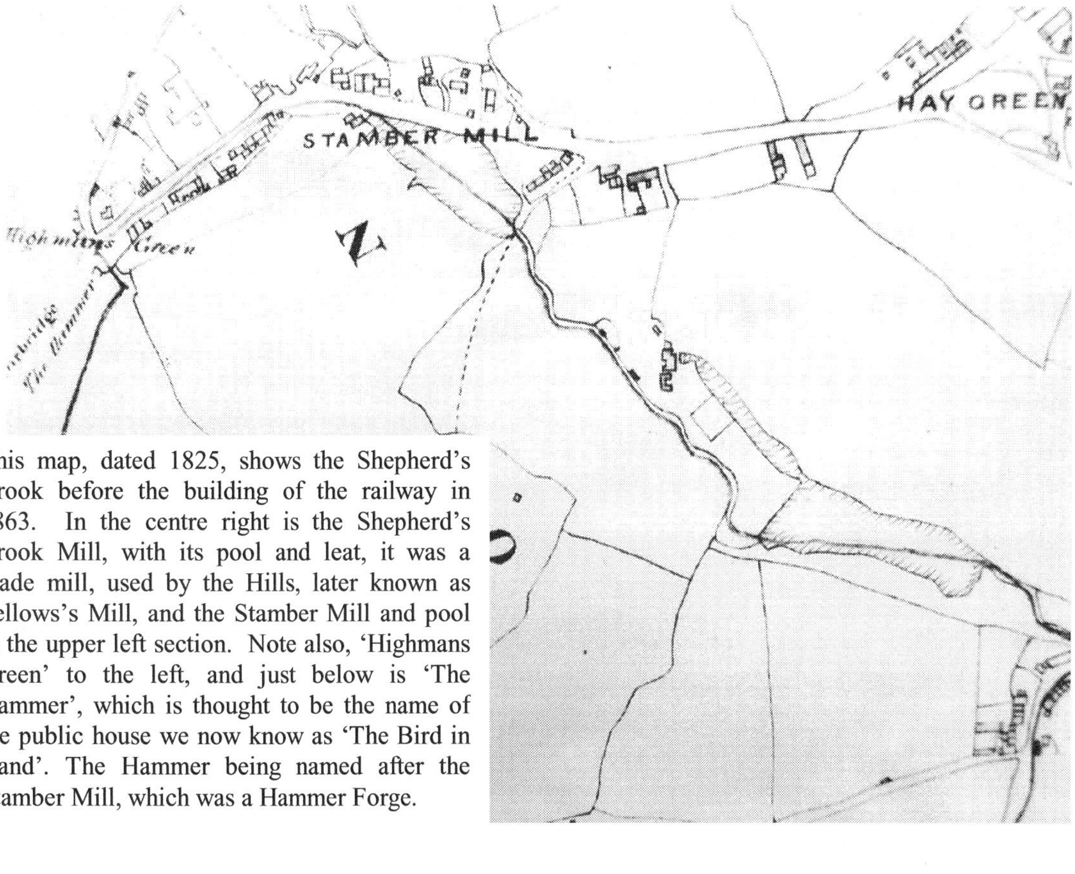

This map, dated 1825, shows the Shepherd's Brook before the building of the railway in 1863. In the centre right is the Shepherd's Brook Mill, with its pool and leat, it was a blade mill, used by the Hills, later known as Fellows's Mill, and the Stamber Mill and pool in the upper left section. Note also, 'Highmans Green' to the left, and just below is 'The Hammer', which is thought to be the name of the public house we now know as 'The Bird in Hand'. The Hammer being named after the Stamber Mill, which was a Hammer Forge.

Stray Hills

A number of stray Hills were found, which could have been part of the family but have not been found a place on the Hill family tree, and were not vigorously researched. One of the most common Christian names being Francis, which can be found dating back to 1550, the other is Waldron, and could only belong to our Hill family (which is probably not strictly true). A number of these names and others are entered below.

A Francis Hill married Sarah Perrins 17th July 1698, at Oldswinford, Sarah was either the daughter of Joseph Perrins, baptised 23rd August 1674, at Oldswinford, or the daughter of John Perrins, baptised 14th March 1674, at Oldswinford.
A Mary Hill was baptised 18th October 1704, at Oldswinford, by Francis and Sarah Hill.

The first Govenor of Oldswinford Workhouse, in 1738, was a John Perrins, who was a nailer, who was assisted by his wife Frances. A John Perrins born 10th July 1682, married Sarah Sidaway, in 1715, who died. He then married Frances Conquest, 6th February 1730. John is probably the father of Joseph Perrins below.

A Joseph Perrins, a nail maker, was appointed Governor of Oldswinford Workhouse in 1783[1]. The Perrinses were shown on Harry Court's map of 1782, living in Perrins Lane, Lye, on a narrow strip of land, where the Perrins family first established their chain making company in 1770. Joseph Perrins married Millicent Knowles, 23rd September 1742; they were the parents of George, who married Sarah Perks from The Hare and Hounds, Careless Green, who were the parents of Thomas Perrins, chain maker, of Careless Green.

Francis Hill baptised 7th April 1550, Belbroughton,
Francis baptised 19th July 1560, Chaddesley, - Peter Hill
Francis baptised 22nd November 1577, Clent, - Abraham & Ann Hill
Francis Hill married Mary Tunkes 30th January 1625, Halesowen
Francis Hill married Suzanna Witton November 1625, Oldswinford
Francis baptised 2nd November 1628, Oldswinford, - Francis Hill
Francis Hill married Elizabeth Muller 4th October 1638, Oldswinford
Francis baptised 21st March 1639, Halesowen, - Francis & Mary Hill
Francis baptised 22nd March 1640, Halesowen, - Francis & Mary Hill
Francis baptised 14th June 1674, Oldswinford, - William Hill
Francis baptised 12th October 1674, Oldswinford, - Joseph Hill
Francis baptised 26th March 1681, Halesowen, - Edward & Joyce Hill

John Hill married Isabell Whitehouse 19th January 1732, Kingswinford
Waldron baptised 3rd June 1739, Kingswinford, - John & Isabell Hill
Waldron baptised 7th May 1740, Kingswinford, - William & Sarah Hill
Waldron baptised 9th May 1775, Oldswinford, - Thomas & Sarah Hill
Waldron baptised 7th May 1797, Oldswinford, - William & Sarah Hill
Waldron baptised 26th December 1806, Oldswinford, - William & Sarah Hill

Waldron Hill married Rachel Reynolds, 1st December 1793, Aston Juxta, B'ham.
Waldron, aged 60, Blacksmith, of Aston, 1881 census, born 1st September 1817 St. Martin's B'ham, of 72 East Side, Aston, married Ann Woodward, 1842, son of above.
Waldron, aged 27, Hairdresser, of Aston, 1881 census, born Birmingham, son of above, married Elizabeth Horrobin, 20th April 1881, St. Saviour, Saltly, Birmingham.
Waldron baptised 1885, Aston, B'ham, - Waldron & Elizabeth Hill, son of above.

[1] See " A HISTORY OF STOURBRIDGE" by Nigel Perry.

Clent Parish Records of Births, Marriages and Deaths, 1561-1837, were transcribed and published in book form in 2006, by the Staffordshire Parish Registers Society. The original records were very patchy, with numerous pages missing, torn, stained and illegible, making it impossible to make a fully joined up Hill family tree.
Other Clent Records taken from the Parish Chest, and mentioned in the book "A Short History of Clent" by John Amphlett, do give further snippets of information about the Hill family and the Church, a few of these are given below.

Clent Church[1] was founded about 1199, and dedicated to Saint Peter and later to Saint Leonard. The first rector was Master Herbert, who was followed by John Waleraund, in 1251, a name thought to be the origin of the name Waldron.
The early roof was covered with shingles made from cleft (riven or split) Oak.

An early mention of the Hills was in 1273, when a list of jurors included 'Richard in the Hull', which was an early development of Surnames from places where people lived, i.e. 'Richard in the Hill', or Richard Hill.
In 1410 a complaint was brought against William Hill of Calcott Hill, for allowing his cattle to graze on land he did not own.

In 1575 Edward Hill is mentioned as being involved in the building of the lychgate, and again in 1595 when, Edward Hill, described as a gentleman, of Calcott Hill, who said he was possessed of a house, and one hundred acres of land in the manor of Church Clent, possibly Calcott Farm. Also mentioned is a field called Halfnell, which could have been another name for Halfmore.

The will of Thomas Hill, a yeoman, who died in 1622, mentions his farm called Austin Jenks, a none existing name in Clent today, which he leased for seven years from Francis Hill for a rent of £25 (a Thomas Hill was buried 23rd August 1621) his stock was valued £144, he is buried beneath the belfry of Clent Church. Richard Hill, who died in 1623, was a tailor, and Francis Hill was a Church Warden in 1623 and Abraham Hill in 1743. Abraham Hill was said to be a nailer.

The first gallery in Clent Church, called "the little gallery above ye south doore", was built in 1675 by twelve parishioners, for their own accommodation, they were Thomas Waldron of Upper Clent – Henry Waldron of Holy Cross – Humphrey Greene of Holy Cross – Gilbert Cole jun. of Holy Cross – John Hill de Oldmill – John Hill of Lower Clent, and Abraham Hill, his brother, Lower Clent – John Hill de Banck, Lower Clent – William Waldron of Lower Clent, and Edward Waldron his brother, Lower Clent – John Hill de Towensend, and Richard Waldron son of Thomas Waldron of Holy Cross. A further gallery, built in 1688, called the "pew that joineth the bell toller built a great while agoe", by Thomas Hill and Henry Cordiwen. In 1715 Thomas Hill sold his five kneelings. This is probably Thomas Hill, father of John Hill of Oldnall. The galleries of Clent Church no longer exist.

In 1778 Mr. Perry assigned one of his kneelings to Mr. Thomas Hill, for his tenant at Halfmore. (This is the Thomas Hill of Coalbournebrook, [1711-1782] who left Halfmore in his will. He also left £5 each to his cousins Thomas Hill [1694], and Richard Hill [1709], at Clent.) [see the family tree on the next page].

---

[1] Map Ref SO 929 793

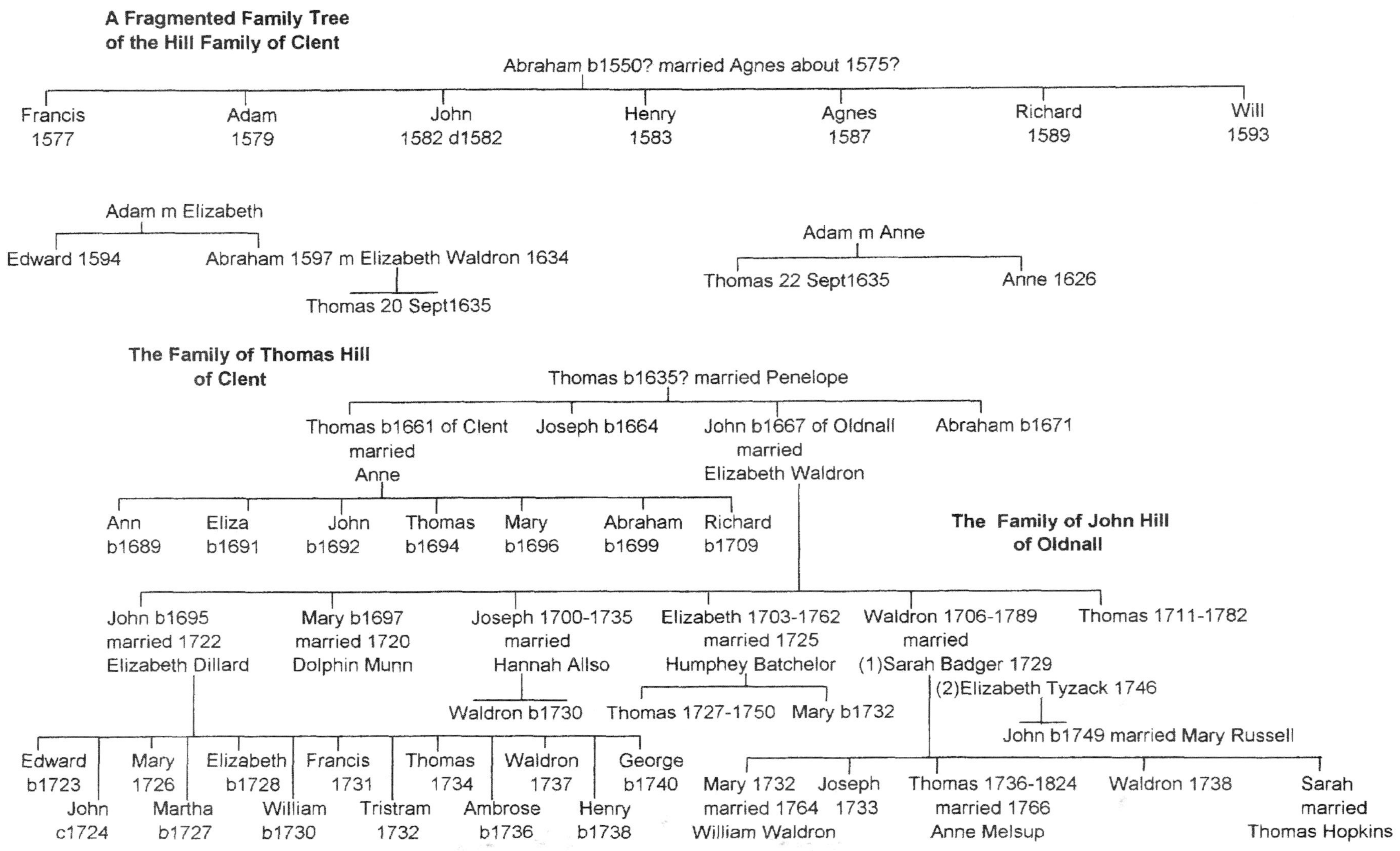
A Fragmented Family Tree
of the Hill Family of Clent
Abraham b1550? married Agnes about 1575?
Francis 1577
Adam 1579
John 1582 d1582
Henry 1583
Agnes 1587
Richard 1589
Will 1593
Adam m Elizabeth
Edward 1594
Abraham 1597 m Elizabeth Waldron 1634
Thomas 20 Sept1635
Adam m Anne
Thomas 22 Sept1635
Anne 1626
The Family of Thomas Hill
of Clent
Thomas b1635? married Penelope
Thomas b1661 of Clent married Anne
Joseph b1664
John b1667 of Oldnall married Elizabeth Waldron
Abraham b1671
Ann b1689
Eliza b1691
John b1692
Thomas b1694
Mary b1696
Abraham b1699
Richard b1709
The Family of John Hill
of Oldnall
John b1695 married 1722 Elizabeth Dillard
Mary b1697 married 1720 Dolphin Munn
Joseph 1700-1735 married Hannah Allso
Elizabeth 1703-1762 married 1725 Humphey Batchelor
Waldron 1706-1789 married (1)Sarah Badger 1729
(2)Elizabeth Tyzack 1746
Thomas 1711-1782
Waldron b1730
Thomas 1727-1750
Mary b1732
John b1749 married Mary Russell
Edward b1723
John c1724
Mary 1726
Martha b1727
Elizabeth b1728
William b1730
Francis 1731
Tristram 1732
Thomas 1734
Ambrose b1736
Waldron 1737
Henry b1738
George b1740
Mary 1732 married 1764 William Waldron
Joseph 1733
Thomas 1736-1824 married 1766 Anne Melsup
Waldron 1738
Sarah married Thomas Hopkins

Wollaston Hall, mentioned in the will of Thomas Hill of Dennis as 'my Capital Mansion'. (Picture from the Stourbridge Library Collection).

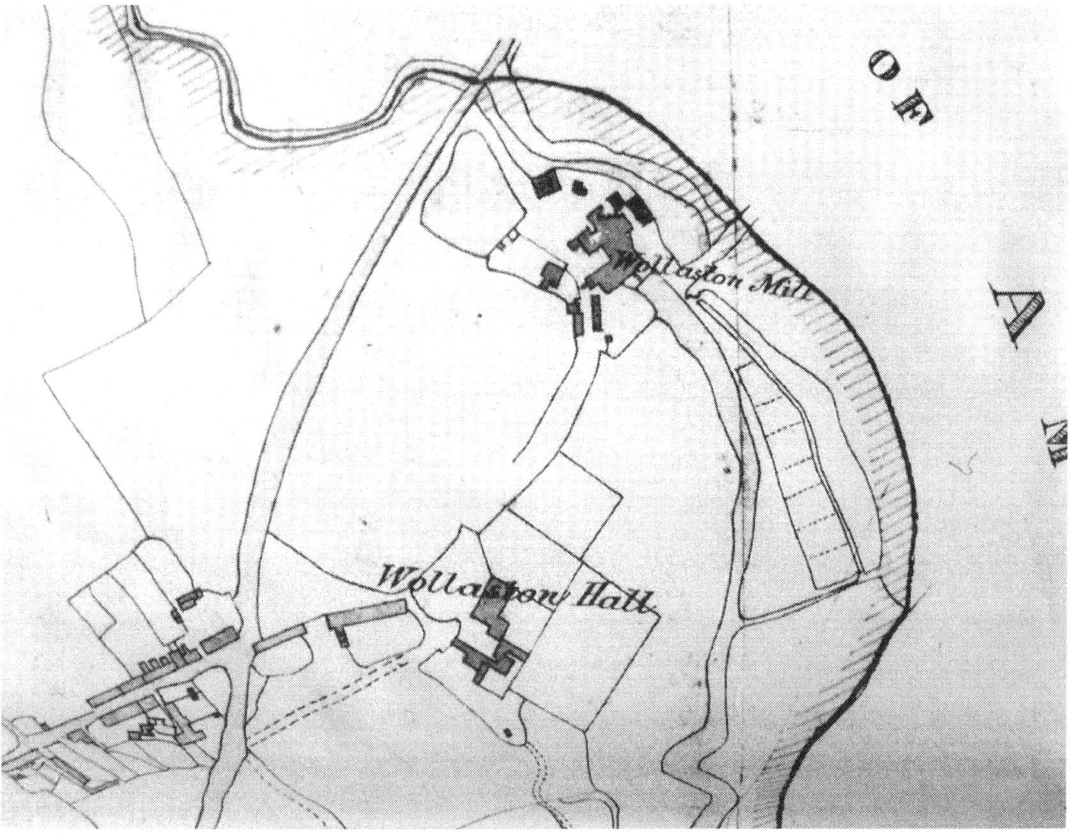

1825 map of Wollaston showing the Wollaston Hall and the Wollaston Ironworks both referred to in the will of Thomas Hill of Dennis.